Victoria & Albert Museum

The Norfolk House Music Room

Desmond Fitz-Gerald

London 1973

Acknowledgements

I am greatly indebted to Mr Francis Steer, the Duke of Norfolk's archivist, Mr Geoffrey Beard, Mr John Cornforth, Mr John Harris, Mr Michael McCarthy, Mr Howard Colvin and my colleagues, Mr Peter Thornton, Mr Simon Jervis and Mr John Hardy, for much information and help in the preparation of this monograph. Thanks are also due to the Soprintendenza ai Monumenti del Piemonte in Turin for assistance in locating photographs. The support given over a number of years by the Marc Fitch Fund to facilitate research in the field of furniture-history is once again gratefully acknowledged.

75p net

Printed in England for Her Majesty's Stationery Office by
Eyre & Spottiswoode Ltd., Thanet Press, Margate K24

SBN 901486 43 4

The Norfolk House Music Room

The association of the Dukes of Norfolk with St James's Square began in 1722, when the trustees of the 8th Duke of Norfolk bought St Albans House on the east side of the square for £10,000. In 1748 the 9th Duke acquired the neighbouring Belasyse House to the north and by September of that year the 'pullying down' of the two old houses was completed. A large site with a frontage of over a hundred feet was now available and the Duke employed Matthew Brettingham the elder to design a new town house fitting for England's premier peer.[1]

Brettingham was the son of a Norwich mason, and had made his reputation as William Kent's assistant at Holkham, which he completed and decorated after Kent's death in 1748. Indeed, Brettingham, when he produced a sumptuous folio on the architecture of Holkham, inscribed his own name as 'Architect' on the plates, making no mention of Kent,[2] and he can be seen in his portrait proudly holding an elevation of Kent's triumphal arch there (pl. 2). Brettingham was, in fact, a humdrum architect who repeated Burlingtonian formulas, and Norfolk House was no exception to the general level of his work. The façade on St James's Square was plain and uninspiring, and in 1771 it was pilloried in the *Critical observations on the buildings and improvements of London*, whose author (probably 'Athenian' Stuart) asks: 'Would any foreigner, beholding an insipid length of wall broken into regular rows of windows, in St James's Square, ever figure from thence the residence of the first Duke of England? "All the blood of the Howards" can never ennoble Norfolk House!'[3] (pl. 3). Though these words are exaggerated, the reticent exterior of Norfolk House gave no hint of the elaboration of the inside. Brettingham's plan (pl. 4) incorporated a grand staircase in the centre of the building, and the layout is obviously derived from the 'family' and 'strangers' wings at Holkham.[4] However, the interior was chiefly remarkable for its magnificent decoration, some of which was purely Kentian, but the most interesting *Régence* and rococo – indeed, Norfolk House, together with the now demolished Chesterfield House, bore the distinction of being one of the first extensive displays of French-inspired decoration in London.

The house and its decoration were completed by February 1756, when Mrs Delany, that inveterate chronicler of eighteenth century tittle-tattle, wrote to her sister: 'The Duke of Norfolk's fine house in St James's Square is finished, and opened to the *grand monde* of London: I am asked for next Tuesday. . .'[5] Unfortunately her description does not survive, but Horace Walpole also went and reported with enthusiasm: 'All the earth was there. You would have thought there had been a comet, everybody was gazing in the air and treading on one another's toes. In short, you never saw such a scene of magnificence and taste. The tapestry, the embroidered bed, the illumination, the glasses, the lightness and novelty of the ornaments and the ceilings are delightful.' He then, in his waspish way, quotes a quip of Lord Rockingham's in reply to someone who had asked him about the reception, 'Oh! there was all the company afraid of the Duchess, and the Duke of all the company.'[6] By an extreme piece of good luck the fullest and most vivid description of this gala recently turned up in a scrapbook formed by William, the elder brother of the famous diarist and Royal Academician, Joseph Farington.[7] It is in a long letter from William dated 'Feb ye 18th 1756' to his sisters, Isabella and Mary, and is of such interest that it is reproduced verbatim in Appendix A, 1. Farington noticed the Music Room as being 'large, wainscotted in a whimsical Taste, the Pannels fill'd with extreem fine Carvings, the Arts & Sciences all gilt, as well as the Ceiling, which was the same design' and it was here that the Duchess sat all evening receiving her guests. It is amusing also to note that Farington took a very dim view of Lady Rockingham, who appeared with no diamonds, obviously intending to show up everyone else who blazed with too many. It was this drum that occasioned one of Richard Owen Cambridge's best parodies – *An Elegy written in an Empty Assembly Room*, which came out the following April. It is the heartfelt cry of Lady Townshend, who had not been invited to Norfolk House by the Duchess, and a few couplets of it are reproduced in Appendix A, 2.

Something must be said here about the character of the Duchess of Norfolk, for, as can be inferred from Lord Rockingham's comment, it was really she who was the dominant figure and patroness over the decoration of the house. Mary, Duchess of Norfolk (pl. 5), was a daughter and co-heiress of Edward Blount, the patron and correspondent of Pope. She was an ardent Catholic and a frequent visitor to France, and it was undoubtedly she who ordered the Continental splendour of the interior of Norfolk House.[8] She is also known to have been something of an

amateur of the arts, and she later designed architectural ornaments and part of the gardens at Worksop, the family house in Nottinghamshire, where she personally supervised much of the decoration.[9]

Norfolk House remained in the possession of the Howard family until 1938, when it was demolished. The Music Room (pl. 1), which was certainly the finest surviving interior, was fortunately saved, and was re-erected in the Museum, complete but for its window wall. The 'Great Drawing Room' of Norfolk House, which William Farington obviously thought the grandest, had had its tapestry removed, and papier-mâché rococo decoration was inserted in the mid-nineteenth century (pl. 8). One of its splendid original door-cases (pl. 45) was acquired by the Museum at a later date (see Appendix D, 1).

The first impression of the Music Room is one of gilded and mirrored splendour that recalls the salons of the *dix-huitième* in Paris. This room has been cited as a primarily rococo interior and Farington found the panelling 'Wainscotted in a whimsical Taste', which clearly suggests a reaction to its foreign appearance. But, on closer inspection, various stylistic problems arise. These problems have frequently been noted, and it has even been suggested that the whole room is a nineteenth century insertion, that the ceiling is composed partly of work from elsewhere, and that all the *boiseries* were imported from abroad.[10] The purpose of this monograph is to analyse the details which have given rise to these suggestions, and to incorporate the extremely important documentation that has recently been brought to my attention by Mr Geoffrey Beard among the Norfolk Mss. at Arundel Castle. In my original article[11] I suggested that some of the *boiseries* in the Norfolk House Music Room were imported from France and matched up in England. This turns out not to have been the case, for the entire bill for the carving and gilding of the main state rooms at Norfolk House has now come to light and this clearly indicates that the work was executed entirely by one John Cuenot, of whom until recently nothing was known. The section of this bill dealing with the Music Room will be fully analysed later, but it shows that Cuenot worked there between March 1753 and February 1756.

In my original article I also tentatively attributed the plasterwork trophies on the Music Room ceiling to the plasterer William Collins, and this now seems to me less likely and I put forward another possible candidate. Most of the rest of the plasterwork was, it was suggested, by Thomas Clarke, because his surname appeared in Matthew

pl. 3   The exterior of Norfolk House, St James's Square, as it appeared
when newly built – a detail from J. Bowles' view of c. 1760. The
Music Room occupied the further three bays on the first floor

Vüe de la Place de S.te Jaques a Londres.

8

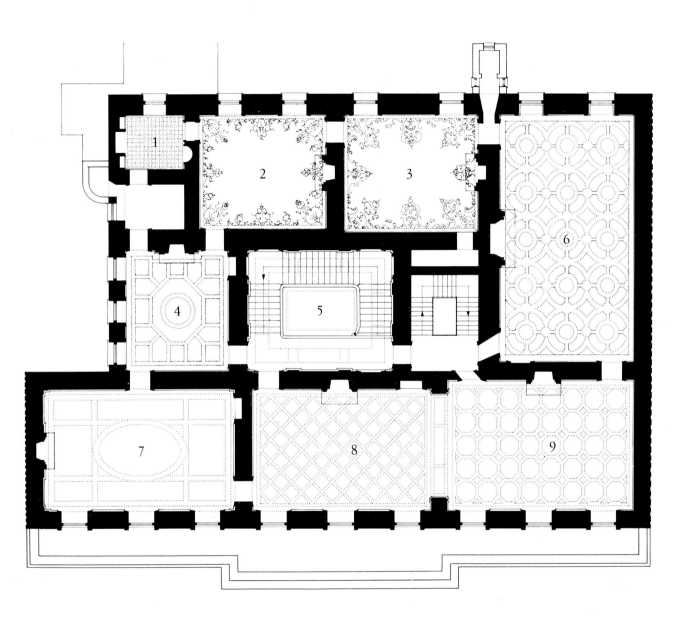

1 China Room or Closet
2 State Dressing Room
3 State Bed Room
4 Ante Room
5 Great Staircase
6 Great Drawing Room or Tapestry Room
7 Music Room
8 Green Damask Room
9 Flowered Red Velvet Room

Brettingham's account book between the years 1748 and 1750.[12] Clarke had been master plasterer to the Office of Works from 1761 to 1782 and had, significantly, worked under Brettingham at Holkham and Euston. This suggestion is now proved without any question, as Mr Beard has also fortunately found a later bill, dated October 1755, for 'Plaisterers Work done for the Duke of Norfolk at his Grace's House in St James's Square', signed and endorsed by Clarke.[13] This document, besides charging £34.13s.9d. for work and repairs on the ground floor, bills £100 'For finishing the Entablet^{re} in great Room according to Mr Bora's Design', and a further £90.13s.11d. is itemized for work done 'In the Principal Floor and part of great Stair Case – Scaffolding, Colouring, and adding to Ornaments – according to Mr Bora's Directions'. This information, coupled with the dates in Brettingham's admittedly cursory account book, shows that the basic structure of the house was completed by 1752, but much of the plasterwork, decoration and carving, in fact all the interior embellishments, continued for another four years. The whole mansion therefore took eight years to completely finish. The last date on Cuenot's bill was February 1756 and this admirably dovetails with the gala mentioned and described by Mrs Delany and William Farington. However, we now have to contend with the new arrival, 'Mr Bora'. What part did he play 'adding to Ornaments' in the decoration of the house and was it he who designed the cartouches in the Music Room which I formerly attributed to Collins? Before answering the second of the two questions, I would like to introduce 'Mr Bora', discuss his style and try to show what he may have been responsible for. Then we must revisit the Music Room and correlate all this new information with my earlier suppositions.

Unlike John Cuenot, a good deal of information is available about Giovanni Battista Borra, the Piedmontese architect who spent parts of a decade or so in England.[14]

Borra was born in 1712, became a pupil of Vittone in Turin, and drew and engraved a number of the plates in Vittone's *Architettura civile* in 1736. He published his *Trattato della cognizione practica delle resistenze* in Turin in 1748, a treatise on engineering problems, and was also responsible for engraved views of that city. In 1750–51 he joined Robert Wood's expedition to Balbec and Palmyra, going in the company of Wood, Dawkins and Bouverie.[15] In Wood's preface to *Palmyra* he stated: 'It was agreed, that a fourth person in Italy, whose abilities, as an architect and draftsman we were acquainted with, would be absolutely

necessary. We accordingly wrote to him, and fixed him for the voyage. The drawings he made, have convinced all those who have seen them, that we could not have employed anybody more fit for our purpose.'[16] The sketchbooks which were the fruit of his work are still extant, together with some of Wood's notebooks about the expedition.[17] Borra returned to England with Wood and Dawkins in the autumn of 1751 and he made in London the enlarged finished drawings from which were engraved the 103 folio plates in the two well-known volumes on Palmyra and Balbec.[18] His only previously known work in England was a 'Palmyra' ceiling for Lord Rivers at Stratfield Saye[19] and his various alterations at Stowe for Earl Temple, where he seems to have been by the end of 1752, but his work on the various garden buildings there has been discussed elsewhere and need not detain us.[20] It is, however, well worth investigating some of the decoration that he carried out in the house, for, as might be expected, he draws much from the wealth of ornamental detail contained in the volumes on Palmyra and Balbec for many of his schemes. The Stowe guide of 1763 is the first to have a 'Description of the Inside of the House': under the entry for the 'State Bedchamber', we find 'The Bed and Ceiling by Signor *Borra*' and 'a very curious Chimney-Piece of White Marble, designed by Signor Borra, and executed by Mr Lovel'.[21] The State Bedchamber (pl. 6), which became in the nineteenth century the Duchess's Drawing-room, is now named the Garter Room, and remains in a much modified state in the present school there. It dates from 1759, and the centre of the ceiling was decorated with the chain and star of the Order of the Garter. Earl Temple had been refused this honour in 1759 but received it in 1760, and the State Bedroom conveniently celebrates his admission to the Order. As might be expected, the frieze and all the decoration on the extremely elaborate ceiling is taken from various plates in Wood's *Palmyra*, and the main motifs are identical to those on the Stratfield Saye ceiling, already mentioned. Borra's state bed, on the other hand, was a gilt domed rococo composition surmounted by a pineapple (pl. 7) It is now in the Lady Lever Gallery, Port Sunlight. Mr George Clark of Stowe informs me that it was put together by Wm Hason 'carpenter' and gilded by John Baptist Dishon in 1759. No carver is mentioned, so presumably it was made in London and sent down to Stowe, where Borra probably supervised Dishon's painting and gilding *in situ*. The mirrors, one of which appears in plate 6, are also

undoubtedly by Borra; a pair survive in a private collection in London and another pair are at Ramsbury in Wiltshire. The 'curious' white chimney-piece in the room was quite unlike contemporary English work and is similar in proportion and design to eighteenth century Turinese examples,[22] a fact easily explained by Borra's origin. This chimney-piece leads us straight back to Norfolk House, for it clearly relates very closely to six chimney-pieces in the various apartments there, including the ones in the Great Drawing Room, Green Damask Room and the Music Room itself (see pls. 8, 9, 10).[23] Their rather low proportions and unorthodox composition are also closely comparable to Turinese examples, such as the one that appears in plate 32, and it would seem more than likely that they were also designed by Borra and possibly even supplied direct to him by the sculptor James Lovel, mentioned in the Stowe guide, for no bills for chimney-pieces survive amongst the Arundel accounts. Lovel turns out to be a substantial figure and will be discussed later in this study.

It is uncertain whether Borra first worked for Earl Temple or the Duke of Norfolk. The surviving Clarke bill of 1755 may well have been the last of a series, for Clarke mentions 'finishing' Borra's entablature in the great room (pl. 8). Borra was probably in on the decoration of the house, since this phase was started in 1752 – the year after Borra's arrival in London, and the date also of his first employment by Earl Temple at Stowe. It is more than likely that the Duke and Duchess were friendly with Temple, for the Norfolks had been very closely associated with the circle of Frederick, Prince of Wales, in the previous two decades. Indeed, they had let the old Norfolk House to him in 1737. This circle, as is now well known, reacted against the rigid Palladianism of Lord Burlington and his followers, and gave much patronage to the rococo painters and craftsmen who so often foregathered at Old Slaughter's Coffee House.[24] Frederick had stayed at Stowe in 1737 as the guest of Lord Temple's uncle, Lord Cobham, a nobleman who had also been an intimate friend and political ally of the Prince. It is not irrelevant to note that Lord Chesterfield, part-creator of those magnificent rococo interiors at Chesterfield House, was another guest during this royal visit. Temple was, furthermore, a cousin of George Lyttleton, the Prince's Secretary and creator of the rococo interiors at Hagley, where we again find the sculptor Lovel working.[25] Lovel had undoubtedly been introduced into this circle by that fashionable 'Goth', Sanderson Miller. Miller's closest friend was Lyttleton, and Miller's

pl. 8 The Great Drawing Room at Norfolk House in 1894, the walls of which were considerably embellished in the early nineteenth century. The chimney-piece, overmantel, door-cases, frieze and ceiling are, however, original. The Italianate chimney-piece can be compared with Borra's example at Stowe (pl. 6). The entablature of the room is 'according to Mr. Bora's (sic) Design'. (*National Monuments Record.* The photo is by Bedford Lemere (12888))

pl. 10 The chimney-piece of the Norfolk House Music Room. The two shown in plates 8 and 9 should be compared with Borra's documented example originally at Stowe (pl. 6) and all here attributed to him

wife was a connection of the Temple family, which could explain Lovel's introduction to Stowe.[26]

Borra's entablature in the Great Drawing Room, or Ball Room as it later became known, already alluded to in Clarke's bill, can be seen in photographs of this room before its demolition (pl. 8). The frieze incorporates acanthus decorated brackets, which do not occur in the two books on Balbec and Palmyra; in fact its composition is rather old-fashioned and it harks back to late seventeenth and early eighteenth century French practice, such as one finds at Versailles, and which was common enough in contemporary Piedmontese interiors. The ceiling above was an exceptionally elaborate series of circles and quadrants. Whether this is also from Borra's design is uncertain. The adjoining drawing-room, called in the eighteenth century the 'Flowered Red Velvet Room', had an octagonal coffered ceiling containing flowered bosses that might have been derived from a plate in *Palmyra*,[27] but, as the neighbouring Green Damask Room (pl. 9), with its lozenge-shaped coffers, was copied from Kent's chapel at Holkham,[28] and the Music Room ceiling (pl. 11) is, apart from its rococo cartouches, clearly based on the engraving of Inigo Jones's ceiling in Whitehall,[29] it therefore seems just as likely that Brettingham may have been responsible for the designing of all of them. Presumably all this plasterwork was carried out by Thomas Clarke and his workmen. In his bill he shows that he used an 'Ornamental Plaisterer' and seven other plasterers, two labourers and two boys. Clarke's bill is, however, more specific about 'part of great Stair Case', which was still visible until demolition (pl. 12), for, though the staircase well had been considerably altered in the 1840s, the upper stage retained its original trophies, Corinthian pilasters, entablature and Kentian bracketed lantern.[30] On the lantern ceiling we find that the Palmyrene pattern of interlaced circles,[31] and the anthemion ornamented frieze itself, which just shows at the top of plate 12, was taken line for line from the same source.[32] Also below the landing appears an enormous double scallop shell of identical cast to those found in the heads of niches at Palmyra.[33] This decoration, therefore, must be due to Borra. However, it is the staircase trophies that really concern us here. They are essentially very baroque compositions of arms and armour, modelled in high relief and each suspended from an ebullient ribbon bow. The trophy on the gallery or west side of the staircase bears considerable resemblance to a trophy, done before Borra's 'Antique' travels, which forms a *cul-de-lampe* to

chapter xxxii of the *Trattato* previously cited (pl. 13), in which he discusses cupolas and lanterns. These staircase trophies are also extremely close to others which appear on the façade of a projected royal palace designed by Vittone and engraved by Borra in 1736 on plate lxxvi of Vittone's *Architettura civile*. The sceptical might point out that many a baroque trophy is of a similar design, but fortunately we can also compare the Norfolk House examples with others designed by Borra in Piedmont in 1756–57, when he was working in his official capacity as architect to the Savoyard Prince, Ludovico Vittorio di Carignano. These trophies appear at the Carignano hunting lodge of Racconigi, south of the Piedmontese capital, where Borra refurbished the interior of Guarini's baroque composition. In the great hall (the Salone d'Ercole) of the palace, which is ceiled by an enormous coffered cove painted in *trompe l'oeil*, the elaborate acanthus brackets of the frieze support little putti heads, details reminiscent of a frieze at Balbec.[34] But the trophies below (pl. 14), fittingly composed with all the attributes of the chase, are again thoroughly baroque in feeling, and the various dead deer, guns, arrows and oak leaves are suspended from almost identical ribbons to those at Norfolk House. The trophies on the Norfolk House staircase are certainly, therefore, from a Borra design.

A further look at the Borra decoration at Racconigi also solves another problem of attribution at Norfolk House. The 'monkey' doors in the Great Drawing Room (pls. 8, 43) are virtually repeated, though here with putti and classical vases in the Sala di Diana, sometimes called the Sala da Riceviménto (pl. 44). On the ceiling of this splendid stuccoed room also appear the same 'Palmyra' interlaced circles that occurred on the staircase lantern at Norfolk House which we noted previously. Thus Borra's responsibility for much of the decoration at Norfolk House becomes more and more evident.

But to return to the Music Room. The magnificent gilt trophies of symbolic objects composed with scrolls, shells, rocaille work and foliage laid into the compartments formed by the ribs decorated with guilloche ornament, inspired by Inigo Jones's ceilings at Whitehall and Greenwich (pl. 11), are lighter in feeling, and originally I thought of them as being designed by another hand. William Farington was clearly thinking of these and the carved musical trophies on the walls and the ceiling plasterwork when he noted the 'extreem fine carvings, the Arts & Sciences all gilt', filling the Music Room (pl. 15).

These cartouches are undoubtedly the most interesting

decoration in the room and are of the highest quality, though their grace and ease are somewhat hampered by the ponderous frame-work that surrounds them. The three panels near the far side-wall are so cramped and awkward that this obviously gave rise to the notion that they originated from elsewhere. They were doubtless 'added ornaments', to re-phrase Clarke's words on his bill, but are they also Borra's work? Their composition is singularly fluid and cursive. These trophies are brilliantly treated and the scrolls, foliage sprays, flowers and rocaille-work must be by the same designer as the delicately drawn rococo ceilings in the old Dining Room (pl. 16) and the State Bedchamber (pl. 17).

This decoration appears to be the work of a plasterer who was also a good sculptor. One has only to glance at the modelling of the magnificent central trophy, complete with Roman breastplate, helmet, spear, bow and quiver – all assembled round a Medusa-headed shield – to realize this (pl. 18). Another superb detail is the painting of Minerva set on an easel in the cartouche representing Wisdom and the art of Painting (pl. 19). Here the sensitivity and freedom of the drawing is especially remarkable. Highly sculptural, too, is another cartouche representing Antique Sculpture, with the appropriate dividers, chisel and mallet round a bust of Seneca (pl. 20), which is taken from either the bronze found at Herculaneum in 1754 (Naples Museum), or an earlier copy of the same model. This latter cartouche and another symbolizing Architecture (pl. 21), charmingly composed with appropriate instruments and a plumb line, around which is folded an accurate plan of Norfolk House (which, incidentally, conveniently disposes of the importation argument), have rocaille frames of C and S curves, cabochons, and shell-work which are very close to the rococo decoration in the other two rooms just mentioned. The question remains whether one can match up all the scintillating rococo plasterwork with contemporary work in England. In my original article I compared the Music Room cartouches to the engraved rococo ceiling designs of Thomas Lightoler (pl. 22),[35] who worked in conjunction with the sculptor and plasterer William Collins. Collins was a pupil of Sir Henry Cheere, and his first documented work dates from 1755.[36] This supposition seemed plausible, as Collins was an intimate of the Old Slaughter's Coffee House in St Martin's Lane.

It was the group at Slaughter's and the St Martin's Lane Academy that was chiefly responsible for the origin of the rococo in England, and the Duchess would have been likely to patronize craftsmen from this circle. It therefore seemed not too rash a guess to put forward the name of William Collins as a possible author of these magnificent plaster trophies and cartouches.

This supposition was reinforced by the fact that Collins was the recipient of several payments 'on acco. of carving' at Worksop, which the Duchess started to reconstruct to James Paine's designs in the years after Norfolk House was completed. Collins must have known the Duchess well, for he sculpted the Worksop pediment to a design from 'her own hand' in 1765. This pediment is fully described and shown in Paine's second volume of *Plans, elevations and sections of Noblemen's Houses*... of 1783 and the rather rococo emblematical composition includes a scroll with a plan of Worksop of similar nature to the Norfolk House example already discussed. Paine also notes her other designs for ornament at Worksop, so it was also within the realms of possibility that the Duchess had a close hand in the ornamentation of the Music Room ceiling.

It would be tempting to have suggested that James Paine might possibly have designed these splendid cartouches himself, for he had studied at the St Martin's Lane Academy – the fountainhead of the English rococo – and his decorative schemes in the Doncaster Mansion House and in various country seats[37] demonstrate his exceptional command of that idiom, before he turned to neo-classicism. Unfortunately, his name does not appear before 1756[38] in any of the Norfolk House or Worksop accounts and this was, as we know, the year that Norfolk House was finished and open for opulent entertaining. However, even Paine's rococo has an Englishness about it, while the Norfolk House work in contrast seems so much more assured and free.

The schizophrenic decoration of the Music Room ceiling is typical of the age that produced it. The rigid Burlingtonians, who stood for Whiggery, disapproved of the rococo: yet it is worth repeating the well-known case of the architect Isaac Ware, who says in his book, *A complete body of architecture*, which came out in 1756, the very year in which Norfolk House was completed: 'It is our misfortune to see at this time an unmeaning scrawl of "C's" inverted, turned, and hooked together, take place of Greek and Roman elegance, even in our most expensive decorations. This is not because the possessor thinks there is or can be elegance in such fond weak ill-jointed and unmeaning figures: it is usually because it is *French*; and fashion commands that whatever is *French* is to be admired as fine:

pl. 16 The ceiling of the downstairs Dining Room at Norfolk House. (*Country Life*)

pl. 17 The ceiling of the State Bedchamber at Norfolk House (*Country Life*). The high rococo decoration of both this and plate 16 closely relates to the Music Room trophies (pls. 18–21) and can be compared to Borra's and Alfieri's ceilings at the Palazzo dell'Accademia Filarmonica in Turin (pls. 23, 25)

pl. 18   The central panel of the ceiling of the Norfolk House Music
Room, showing a martial trophy which, with the other ornaments in
the ceiling panels, is attributed to Borra and was possibly executed by
James Lovel

pl. 19   The section of the Music Room ceiling emblematic of Painting.
A panel with a representation of Minerva stands on the easel

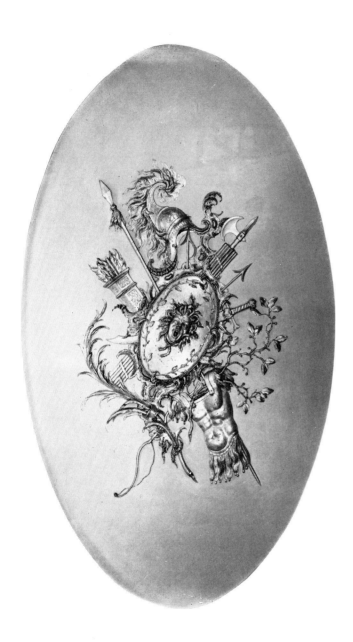

pl. 20 A magnificent rococo composition in the Music Room representing Sculpture including sculptor's tools grouped around an antique head of Seneca

pl. 21 In this representation of Architecture in the Music Room, the curling roll of paper shows a ground plan of Norfolk House

pl. 22 (below) A rococo cartouche by Thomas Lightoler comparable in outline to those in plates 20 and 21

the two words (so Low are the Britons sunk) mean the same thing!' These fulminations against the rococo hardly seem compatible with the views of his friends at Slaughter's Coffee House;[39] in fact he was a fellow-traveller living in both worlds and it is probable that Brettingham adopted a similar stance. It was certainly for political reasons that Ware attacked the rococo – the Seven Years' War with France started in 1756, the year of Ware's publication; similarly Thomas Johnson, that creator of vivid rococo mirrors and rococo furniture, dedicated his book of designs to Lord Blakeney, the Grand President of the Anti-Gallican Association.[40] These artists were in fact trying to make the rococo a respectable style for the English architect and designer. It is, moreover, surely more than a coincidence that all the houses where rococo decoration is to be found – Woodcote, Belvedere, Hagley, Chesterfield and Norfolk House – were owned by proprietors who were anti-Burlingtonian, friends of Frederick, Prince of Wales, and (at some time) members of the Opposition; the set, in fact, of which Mary, Duchess of Norfolk, was an important member.

Collins was a reasonable suggestion as the sculptor connected with the Decoration of the Music Room, but unfortunately there is nothing concretely comparable to the Norfolk House rococo work to justify the claim. It was, however, in character that the Duchess favoured a foreign architect-designer such as Borra. Borra, too, in typical eighteenth century fashion, though fresh from academic investigations of Roman antiquities, did not hesitate to revert to his baroque background and use the Continental rococo for the chimney-pieces, wall decoration and bed that he designed during his stay in England. It seems more than certain that Borra designed and supervised all the high rococo decoration for the Duchess.

The most important clue to this supposition is that English contemporary rococo plasterwork is much more halting and fragmented. As has been said, Paine's compositions are stiffer and less assured in comparison to the truly Continental flavour of the borders and centre-pieces of the Norfolk House downstairs Dining Room and first floor State Bedchamber (pls. 16, 17), not to mention the Music Room cartouches themselves. These swirling compositions relate far more closely to Turinese rococo decoration, and the ceilings of the Palazzo dell'Accademia Filarmonica (pl. 23), where Borra was working intermittently with Benedetto Alfieri from before his middle eastern travels, in 1740 till after Alfieri's death in 1767,[41]

can be cited immediately. They show Borra's fully developed high rococo style and the comparison is obvious.

The only other comparable rococo decoration in England occurs in two places. Firstly at Stratfield Saye, where, as has been said, he designed the 'Palmyra' ceiling of the dining-room for Lord Rivers. The drawing-room there (pl. 24) has a slightly coved cornice with delicate garlands and rocaille corner-cartouches, and the ceiling with its centre sunburst chandelier boss and boldly cursive C and S curves, some bound with ribbon, like the Stowe bed, directly relates to another (pl. 25) at the Palazzo dell' Accademia Filarmonica. It seems, therefore, that Borra must again have been the designer. Secondly there is another 'Palmyra' ceiling at Woburn Abbey in Queen Victoria's Bedroom. Horace Walpole noticed it in October 1751 as being 'after Palmyra'.[42] This is a remarkably early reference, as Borra, Wood and Dawkins only arrived back in London precisely then. This very fact might suggest that Borra's drawing for plate xix in *Palmyra* must have been made available to the Duke of Bedford immediately. It would seem unlikely that Henry Flitcroft, architect of the rebuilding of Woburn, would have had access to it otherwise. This, coupled with the fact that very fine rococo plasterwork decorates the Yellow Drawing Room and Prince Albert's Dressing Room in the North wing of Woburn, makes one speculate as to whether Borra was not called in to do all this decoration. The plasterwork of the ceiling of the Yellow Drawing Room (pl. 26) is extremely close to Stratfield Saye (pl. 24) and Norfolk House (pl. 16) and, as the decoration of these rooms continued through the fifties, the dates are not inconsistent with Borra's English visit or visits.[43] This new Woburn attribution has to remain in the realms of speculation, as no mention of Borra has been found in the surviving accounts.[44] Nor for that matter have any accounts been found for the decoration and plasterwork of these rooms.

After this digression to Stratfield Saye and Woburn we must return to the Norfolk House decoration: having now doubted Collins's participation, it seems worth putting forward another tentative candidate.

James Lovel's name has already been touched upon and it has been suggested that he carved the Norfolk House chimney-pieces for Borra. Borra may have met Lovel at Stowe, where the latter worked very extensively for Lords Cobham and Temple from 1747 to 1777.[45] Lovel, according to Gunnis, was a protégé of Horace Walpole and he sculpted various funerary monuments during the fifties and

pl. 23 Rococo plasterwork designed by Borra and Alfieri in the gallery of the Palazzo dell'Accademia Filarmonica in Turin. (This and plates 25, 32 and 44 are reproduced by kind permission of the Soprintendenza ai Monumenti del Piemonte)
pl. 24 Rococo plasterwork, probably by Borra, on the ceiling of the Drawing Room at Stratfield Saye. (*National Monuments Record*)

sixties.[46] This neglected figure can probably only be properly studied after a close perusal of the Stowe accounts in the Henry E. Huntington Library at San Marino, California,[47] but the most significant thing about Lovel is that, besides being an established sculptor in marble, he also worked in plaster and papier-mâché. For instance, he modelled a Jacobean style 'Good King James Gothick' ceiling pendant to Miller's design for Lord North's hall at Wroxton Abbey in 1752,[48] and in the same year Lord North's father, Lord Guilford, wrote from Waldershare in Kent to Miller saying 'Will you be so good as to put Mr Lovel in mind he was to put another rose on my ceiling?'[49] Further interior work, including the chimney-pieces, was designed and executed by him under Miller's superintendence at Belhus, Lord Dacre's seat in Essex,[50] and Bishop Pococke mentioned in 1756 a statue of Caractacus that Lovel had carved for Lord Guilford to give to Miller for his garden at Radway, in Warwickshire, calling the sculptor-plasterer, 'a countryman of great genius now established in London'.[51] Therefore he would have been settled in London by the time Norfolk House was being fitted up. It is then a considerable temptation to suggest that this sculptor-plasterer might have executed the Music Room trophies and the other rococo decoration at Norfolk House to Borra's orders as a result of their previous collaboration on Stowe.

To return to the ceiling, four of the cartouches of which have already been discussed. The others represent Literature, Astronomy, Music, Geometry and Surveying and are laid out in the following manner:

	Door	
Music	Painting	Literature
Sculpture	⬭	Architecture
Astronomy	Surveying	Geometry

Fireplace (left side), *Door* (right side top and bottom)

An elaborate acanthus frieze inset with cabochons completes the plaster decoration. It is probably the work of Clarke and his team.

Having discussed the two styles of plasterwork on the

Norfolk House Music Room ceiling and noted that its chimney-piece, like others in the house, was probably designed by Borra, we should now sketch in the known facts about John Cuenot and investigate his extensive bill 'for Sundry Articles of Work done and Goods delivered from March 5th 1753 to February 24th 1756'. The section relating to the Music Room is reproduced *in toto* in Appendix B, and the heading and a portion of his bill is illustrated in plates 27 and 28.

Cuenot's name appears mis-spelt as 'Ceunot' in Gunnis's *Dictionary of British sculptors*, where it is stated that he was the son of a French sculptor with the same Christian name, and where mention is made of the younger Cuenot receiving a premium from the Society of Arts in 1762.[52] There are, however, several references to Cuenot, father and son, in the primary source of reference on the Society of Arts premiums, Robert Dossie's *Memoirs of agriculture and other oeconomical arts* of 1782.[53] Under the list of 'Premiums bestowed in Polite Arts' for 'Modelling Bas Relief Ornaments in Clay, Flowers and Foliage for Festoons, under 19 Years; Birds and Beasts, for Frizes and Tablets under 22 Years...' we find young Cuenot described as 'taught by his Father' and 'Carver since dead'. He won premiums for festoons in 1762 and 1763. It is the father who concerns us here. Also in the list we find that 'John Scott. Apprentice of Cuenot. Sen' won premiums for festoons in 1760. This is proof that John Cuenot senior must have had a workshop; in the same list other winners are mentioned as being apprenticed to such important names in the history of the English rococo as Cheere, Roubiliac, Carter and Moser. In Gunnis's Ms. additions to his *Dictionary*, John Cuenot is noted as being paid £6.19s. in 1751 by the statuary Thomas Carter.[54] These facts, coupled with the information that as a 'Carver' and 'Framemaker' he was paid small sums by the Dukes of Northumberland and Montagu in 1752[55] and 1759,[56] respectively, suggest that John Cuenot was an extremely well-known craftsman in his day. Mortimer's *Universal directory* of 1763 lists a 'Cuenot – carver, Warwick Street, Golden Square'.[57] From this address it was possible to check the Westminster rate-books[58] and Cuenot, variously mis-spelt, appears as having lived in the street between 1744 and 1762, when the word 'Dead' was written opposite his name. His son was there in 1763, obviously subscribing to Mortimer after his father's death, and in 1764 he, too, was dead, for a new rate-payer had taken over the premises, which fits in with Dossie's previously quoted mention of the younger Cuenot being 'since dead' in that year. A rent

pl. 25   Another ceiling in the Palazzo dell'Accademia Filarmonica comparable to that in plate 24

pl. 26   The Yellow Drawing Room at Woburn Abbey (*Country Life*). It is tentatively suggested that Borra may also have designed the rococo ceiling here.

pls. 27 & 28   The heading and a section from John Cuenot's bill for the carving done at Norfolk House

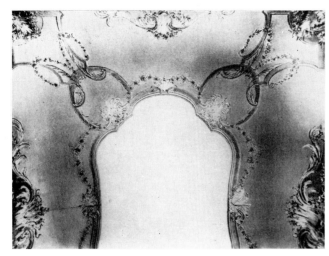

His Grace The Duke of Norfolk .... Dr

To John Cuenot for Sundry Articles of Work done, & Goods delivered, from March 5th 1753 to Feb. 24 1756. viz.

Musick Room

To carving 9 heads with various Ornaments to fold over mouldings with flowers & 4 modillions	21. 3. —
To carving the Ornaments over 3 Doors	30. 10. —
To carving 6 Trophies to go in the pannels with laurels & oak branches	60. 5. —
To carving 4 large foldridge leaves for Do	16. 16. —
To carving 8 Ears for Do	8. 18. —
To 8 Branches of flowers for Do not design'd in the Drawing	4. 2. —
To carving the Ornaments of 6 less pannels with foldridge & flowers	39. 12. —
To carving the sides of two Glass frames with flowers folding over sticks	16. 9. —
To carving the two bottoms of Do not expres'd in the Drawing	6. 15. —
To carving 54 foot of Ruffled leaf & stick for the Window Cornishes @ 1 d ⅌ foot	2. 14. —
To 54 foot of long water leaf for Do @ 1. 5 ⅌ foot	3. 16. 6
To 54 foot of Bead beaded @ 5 d ⅌ foot	1. 2. 6
To making the Scrowls of Do & to four large pannels at the top & bottom & to the top of the two Glasses	9. 8. —
To making the mouldings of 5 pannels and the top of 2 Doors which makes 16 pieces	0. 12. —
To carving an Ornament to cover the joint of the Chimney Glass	4. 18. —
carried forward £	235. 1. —

28

of £18 a year was paid for the workshop, an amount much the same as for the other houses in this street. In contrast to these documented facts, it is worth indulging in a little speculation about the French background of John Cuenot, for it cannot but be significant that he signed himself 'Jean Antoine Cuenot' on the receipts for his Norfolk House work.[59]

A family named Cuenot appears to have originated from Doubs in the Franche-Comté, the first recorded of which was called Jean Cuenot, a locksmith (*serrurier*) in Ornans during the late sixteenth century.[60] The best known member of this family was the sculptor, architect and engineer François Cuenot, who was born in about 1610 and had established himself in Savoy by 1638, when he was working at Chambéry for the Dukes of Savoy. He seems to have carved in wood and, significantly, specialized in *boiseries*, becoming in 1660 *sculpteur* to Charles Emanuel II of Savoy. He later published a book of architecture and, during the last years of his life, seems to have specialized in bridge building. A son, Pierre-François, followed in his father's footsteps.[61] There is, as yet, no proof that our Jean-Antoine Cuenot was a relation of this family, but the name was far from common, and his signature, coupled with the fact that he uses the French word *trumo* for pier glasses and *montons* (the French *montant*) for the fillet placed over the joints of mirror plates, consistently throughout his bill, indicates French origin. This, together with the French or Piedmontese character of the mirrors throughout the main Norfolk House state rooms, makes it likely that he was an immigrant Frenchman, possibly of the same family. Charles Emanuel II of Savoy was the father of Victor Amadeus, first King of Sardinia, so that a link with the Piedmontese Borra fits in satisfactorily, which point raises the question of Borra's part in the design of the woodwork at Norfolk House.

In the detailed account for the Music Room, Cuenot specifies particular details 'not designed' and 'not express'd in the Drawing'. This shows in the most concrete way that a set of master drawings must have existed, and this, together with Thomas Clarke's mentions of 'Mr Bora's Directions' and 'Designs', gives strong grounds for supposing that Borra designed most of the ornamentation inserted in the Burlingtonian framework of Brettingham's room and his compartment ceiling in the style of Inigo Jones.

The 'glass frames' or pier-glasses (pl. 29) between the windows in the Music Room (those on the wall not re-erected in the Museum) were vertically framed by flanking pilasters composed of 'flowers folding over sticks'. Borra's Stowe State Bed (pl. 7) has four bed-posts with similar bundles of sticks, though bound, in this case, with ribbon, and the bed canopy is composed with large and elaborate acanthus sprays, not unlike those that centre the lower portion of the chimney-glass and panels in the Music Room (pl. 15) and which, again, relate to others on top of the chimney-glass in the Great Drawing Room (pl. 8).[62]

The treatment of the elaborately carved, fronded decoration of the Music Room pier-glasses, which stood on a Vitruvian-scrolled plinth over the dado, is similar to that of the base of the mirrors in the Gallery of the Palazzo dell'Accademia Filarmonica in Turin, the interior of which we know was designed by Borra in collaboration with Benedetto Alfieri.[63] (There were also mirrors similarly treated in the Green Drawing Room, which was next door to the Music Room in Norfolk House (pl. 30)).

In Cuenot's bill, puzzlingly, it is the lower portion of the Music Room window-mirrors that were 'not express'd in the Drawing', so it is still by no means clear exactly what part Borra played in the design of the ornament in the room. It is certainly true to say that, if one compares the window pier-glasses (pl. 29) with those of the overmantel (pls. 1 and 15) and the other large panels in the room (pl. 31), one is immediately struck by the less sophisticated general proportions and more halting profile of the panels. These are not composed with the stick-and-garland surround that forms undulating ears flanking the musical trophies on the pier-glasses. All the other main panels of the room including the overmantel mirror, have voluted ears running up to acanthus brackets, which in turn support the final scrolls on either side of the masks. Borra may have designed only the window-mirrors, perhaps only supplying a general sketch for the other panels, leaving Cuenot to work out the details of the carved work of these panels and the way in which they were to be fitted into the architectural confines of the room.

Again, if one looks to Turin, it is possible to find a significant parallel to this less successful wall treatment. Plate 32 shows the decoration of the lower part of the fireplace-wall of a room in the Palazzo Carignano and, though we do not know if this was designed by Borra, it is in the palace of his patron Ludovico Vittorio, so the suggestion is not too far-fetched. The panelling here is far more sophisticated, but the typical Turinese chimney-piece – itself very close to the Norfolk House Music Room example

– supports a frond-centred composition, flanked by panels, that seems to be an urbane echo of the Music Room treatment.

Cuenot's bill clearly highlights the room's most expensive items: nine 'Heads', or masks, which included five on the three pelmet-boards and pier glasses – on the window wall not erected in the Museum – came to £21.3s.od. These espagnolettes (pls. 33, 34) are derived, together with their flanking volutes, from motifs commonly found in the engraved work of Jean Bérain (pls. 35, 36).[64] It is curious, though, how they differ, for those over and opposite the chimney-glass (pl. 33) are in a cosmopolitan late Louis XIV style and well supported in a cartouche that satisfactorily links itself to the flanking volutes. All the others (pl. 34), and this includes those on the window wall, are of much cruder quality: they are heads which one would expect to find on an English console-table in the style of William Kent, and they seem awkward and adrift in their space, being unlinked to their volutes or to the knot of the ribbon below them. These volutes, too, do not have the deeply incised verve of the others. These marked differences in carving suggest that Cuenot employed both French and English carvers in his workshop, or perhaps even executed two sections himself, leaving the rest to his underlings.

His bill only mentions 'ornaments over three doors', at £30.10s.od. Now the pair of doors opposite the chimney-piece (pl. 37) have a surmounting panel decorated with acanthus and scroll-work identical to the lesser panels of the room, while over the central door appears an elaborately entwined monogram capped by a ducal coronet (pl. 38).[65] This would certainly have been specified in Cuenot's bill had he executed it; it must, therefore, date from a later period, when the Great Drawing Room, on the same floor, had similar motifs placed over its 'monkey' doors (pl. 43).

The most expensive single charge in the Music Room bill was £60.5s.od., for the series of six trophies of musical instruments 'to go on the panels with laurels and oak branches'. They are of superlative quality and of typical early eighteenth century French design and, to illustrate this, it is worth comparing one of these (pl. 39) with an engraving after Jacques-François and Marie-Michelle Blondel by Jacques Dumont (le Romain) (pl. 40).[66] They were probably designed by Borra, for they can be compared with his other trophies reproduced in plates 12, 13 and 14; for instance, the elaborately knotted ribbons, the fronds of laurel leaves and pendant swag of material constantly recur. Also, in the next-door Green Damask Room, the

'Mathematical Trophies', as Cuenot termed them, on the pier-glasses (pl. 30), and the overmantel mirror (pl. 9), are all symbolic of architecture and composed with set-squares, dividers and quill pens, quite similar to the head-piece of Borra's preface to his *Trattato* already mentioned (pl. 41). Beneath the trophies on the three interior walls of the Music Room, and centring the base volutes of the four large panels, sprout robust fan-shaped acanthus sprays. Cuenot terms them '4 large foldridge leaves' and charged four guineas each for them. The chimney- and pier-glasses, and the large panels of the room, were each flanked and lit with '12 Double Branches with Nozels, Sockets and pans'. These twiggy creations are ingeniously carved out of wood and strengthened inside with wire. After the trophies, they were the room's most expensive items, running to £57.12s.od. The nozzles and drip-pans have recently been restored in composition, the originals having been lost (pl. 42).

The total sum for all the carving and gilding work was £647.7s.3d., making the Music Room the most expensive scheme that Cuenot worked on at Norfolk House. For instance, the decoration of the Green Damask Room next door was a little over half the price at £382.8s.4d. These high prices are easily explained, for all the walls of the other rooms on the *piano nobile* were decorated with damask or tapestries rather than elaborately carved panelling.

There is nothing rococo about these panels; they are far more *Régence* in character and must have seemed old-fashioned compared to the contemporary rococo *boiseries* in the Drawing Room at Chesterfield House. They certainly do not live up to the ceiling decorations at Norfolk House.

The composition and treatment of this panelling have a couple of parallels in the British Isles, where it is far more common to find such decoration done in stucco-work.

An approximately similar treatment in plasterwork occurs as far afield as on the staircase of no. 86 St Stephen's Green, in Dublin,[67] and, before its demolition, in the Dining Room at Halnaby.[68] The influence probably derived from Norfolk House, which in turn has its connections with the Palazzo Carignano decoration possibly by Borra previously mentioned.

The meticulous detail of Cuenot's bill is of particular interest: for instance, all the various kinds of moulding used have different terms, such as 'Bubble and floroon', 'Ribbon and Stick' and 'Beads and Pearls'. The fact that he talks of 'french Eggs and Darts' as opposed to 'italion

pl. 30   The 'glass frames' and console-tables of the Green Damask
Room, which was next door to the Music Room at Norfolk House.
(*Country Life*)

foldridge' obviously reflects his Continental background. An English clerk must have made up the bills, for the writing is quite unlike Cuenot's own hand, which appears on his own receipts. One such receipt shows that he received one thousand pounds 'in part of money due to me from his Grace', on 25 October 1756. The bill was evidently checked and double-checked by the Duke's man-of-business, Anthony Wright, for an error of seven pence was found, the bill being then meticulously altered.[69]

A set of bills from other tradesmen has recently been discovered among the Norfolk Mss. at Arundel, and, though Cuenot's bill heads the list with more than double the money set out in any of the others, large sums were charged by the upholsterer Joseph Metcalfe, the carpenter William Edwards, the painter, the glazier, etc., etc.[70] Most tantalizing of all is the fact that the bill of Saunders and Bradshaw, the well-known firm of upholsterers and cabinet-makers, is alone missing from the pile.[71] William Edwards' bill for the 'carpenters and joyners Work' makes it quite clear that 'the ornaments of Chimney and Pier-glass and Table Frames' in the main rooms – Cuenot's work in fact – was quite separate, and in his bill he charged £120.12s.0d. for work in the Music Room. One item shows that Edwards prepared the pier-glasses and frames for Cuenot to carve as early as 1753. Elsewhere he mentions polishing the mahogany doors and putting up a shelf in the closet behind the dummy door that balances its mate and leads to the Green Damask Room (pl. 37). He also laid the floor and provided scaffolding and other essential equipment.

The painter's bill from George Evans in 1755 shows that the Music Room was done with 'clear cold white lead [paint] twice in Oil Dead White'. This background to the room's gilt decoration would have created a far more glittering effect than that given by the present mottled cream colour. The taste for white and gold decoration had become popular at Versailles under Louis XIV, and Horace Walpole in Paris in December 1765 remarks: 'I have seen but one idea in all the houses here; the rooms are white and gold, or white; a lustre, a vast glass over the chimney, and another opposite, and generally a third over against the windows compose their rooms universally.'[72] So the colour of the Music Room was fashionable by French standards, even if the panelling itself was out of date when compared with the advanced (for England) rococo woodwork of Chesterfield House.

The white marble chimney-piece of the Music Room (pl. 10) has already been touched upon in connection with

Borra's documented example formerly in the Garter Room at Stowe. Both in proportion and decorative detail, this resembled those in the Norfolk House Green Damask Room and Great Drawing Room and the Music Room itself. As all of these are comparable to other Piedmontese examples in the Royal Palace and in the Palazzo Carignano (pl. 32) and Palazzo dell'Accademia Filarmonica in Turin,[73] it is logical to attribute the design of the Norfolk House series to Borra and the execution to Lovel. The decorative motifs on the Music Room chimney-piece, such as the frieze blocks carved with musical trophies, the scrolls centring on an Aurora mask, the acanthus leaves and the pendant garlands, clearly echo the decoration of the room, which again supports Borra's participation in the overall design of Cuenot's woodwork.

The finest of the mantelpieces designed by Borra at Norfolk House was the one in the Great Drawing Room (pl. 8), the carved marble festoons of which Farington likened to the work of Grinling Gibbons. The definition and crispness of its carving, judging from this late nineteenth century photograph of the room and another in the National Buildings Record by Bedford Lemere, shows Farington to have been quite justified in his comparison. Certainly the quality of the Music Room example is much below this standard. In fact the carving is lifeless and sludgy and it is not altogether surprising that many have previously considered it to be a nineteenth century addition. It probably represents the work of another sculptor working to Borra's design, possibly in Lovel's workshop.

Farington's letter brings up another lacuna in the house accounts, for, when he describes the Great Drawing Room, he claims that the glasses cost 'a thousand [pounds] being the largest plates, I fancy that were ever brought over', going on to say, 'but throughout ye whole house the glass is thought the most remarkable furniture.' The mirrors were, of course, imported, like the tapestries, from France and probably originated from St Gobain in Picardy, as such large plates were not manufactured in England until a few years after the Ravenhead works had been founded in 1773. Cuenot's bill starts with accounts for silvering small pieces of glass and includes an entry for a plate 43½ × 22 inches, 'cut in two' in the Music Room. These were presumably used in the mirror borders. The large pieces must have cost a great deal and may have been supplied direct from France. Here it can be recorded that in 1773, when the Northumberlands imported their great mirrors for the Glass Drawing Room at Northumberland

pl. 31   A section of the panelling in the Norfolk House Music Room
pl. 32   A chimney-piece and portion of the wooden panelling in the
Palazzo Carignano in Turin which has close affinities with the
chimney-piece and panels of the Music Room

House, they ordered theirs through an upholsterer, even trying to evade the exorbitant seventy-five per cent duty on mirror glass by unsuccessfully attempting to get them smuggled in.[74] The Duchess of Northumberland, when visiting the state rooms of the German palace of Ludwigsburg, remarked: 'In one of them there is a large looking glass in which they greatly pride themselves, it is about the size of those of Norfolk House.'[75] So the famous Norfolk House mirrors may well have influenced the Northumberlands to out-do them in Adam's fashionable neo-classical scheme at Northumberland House, a section of which, by ironic chance, is also in this Museum.

The decoration of the Music Room having now been considered, it only remains to talk about its furnishings. Regrettably, as has been said, Saunders and Bradshaw's bill is missing, and so there is no way of knowing what they supplied – tapestries, upholstery or furniture. Cuenot's bill includes gilding and painting eighteen stools in the Music Room, but presumably these were already in the house. Cuenot very seldom executed seat furniture, confining himself practically always to fixtures. For instance, in the Green Damask Room he carved the console-tables under the mirrors, or 'trumos' as he always called them, between the windows (pl. 30), and on the staircase he executed the splendid eagle-crested lanterns over the doors (pl. 47), all of which remained in situ until the sale in 1938. As these are fully documented, the bills for them are reproduced in Appendix D. Elsewhere in his bill, Cuenot mentions supplying other elaborate tables, picture-frames, and girandoles. Only three stools and one 'pattern Chair' are charged for.

Joseph Metcalfe's bill for upholstery is dated 9 May 1752, and the contents, which include supplying 'India damask' wallpaper, furniture covers and curtains, may well represent work done before Borra was brought in, early in 1752.[76] Presumably Metcalfe was replaced by Saunders and Bradshaw and, if their bill had survived, we might have a clearer picture of the furnishings. However, this loss is partially overcome by the discovery of an undated 'Inventory of Furniture in St James's Square when rebuilt and new furnish't', which must, from its title, date from after the opening of the house in 1756.[77] This deals with every room in the house from cellar to garret and shows exactly what was in the Music Room when newly opened (see Appendix C). In connection with decoration, the inventory lists the '2 Large pier Glasses', which are those between the windows, and 'A Large Glass over Chymney',

but the fourth one (pl. 37), now between the doors, is not mentioned at all. If one refers back to Cuenot's bill, nothing is said of this mirror either, whereas Cuenot is quite specific in charging for 'carving an Ornament to cover the joint of the Chimney Glass'. As these identical fillets or joints of the fourth mirror were not indicated, it becomes clear that what was originally a plain panel must have been ingeniously transformed into a mirror at a later date. This suggestion is supported by a later inventory of Norfolk House dating from 1777 (see Appendix C), taken after the Duke's death,[78] which even lists the size of the mirror plates of the pier- and chimney-glasses, but again does not support the existence of a fourth mirror.

Cuenot's '12 Double Branches' appear in the first inventory as '6 pr. Rich Double Arms Gilt' and his pelmet boards enclosed '3 green and silk Damask w^{do} [window] Curtains…' These would have been pull-up curtains, worked by pulleys and cords and moving up behind the draped pelmet itself. Plate 29 shows later replacements in the form of three pairs of curtains which awkwardly conceal the carved window architraves. The fact that pairs of curtains are not mentioned in the inventory is a further indication that single pull-up curtains existed, and in plate 29 one of the hooks for the original cords can just be seen on the right-hand architrave of the central window. The original effect, but not of course the material, survived in the Green Damask Room next door to the Music Room, and these pull-up curtains can plainly be seen in plate 30. The inventory also mentions '3 brown holland Spring curtains', which were spring-blinds to keep out the sun and were similar to those we have today. What function the '4 brass rods down the sides' fulfilled is not clear, though the brass rods before the pier-glasses were obviously put there 'to prevent people coming too near' and therefore to protect the carving and mirror plates from the throngs of visitors that passed through the room at parties such as that which William Farington so graphically describes.

The rest of the furnishing of the room seems to have been very sparse, comprising little more than three card-tables. Two of these are described as with 'Compass fronts'. This means that they were struck out with a compass or, in other words, that they were of curved or serpentine shape. Somewhat incongruously, a mahogany dining-room table is listed. This was almost certainly a folding table: it may have been in the room by chance when the inventory was made, or it may have lived in a cupboard masked by one of the false doors. Fourteen, rather than Cuenot's eighteen,

pls. 33 & 34   Differing 'Heads' or masks, from over the chimney-
glass and over a panel in the Music Room

pl. 37 The Music Room showing the wall opposite the chimney-piece, which consists of a dummy door on the left, and its mate to the right, which originally led into the Green Damask Room. They flank a glass which, from interpreting Cuenot's bill and the inventories, turns out to be a later insertion

stools make their appearance, though these are better described in the 1777 inventory (see Appendix C), which shows that seven were long stools of various lengths and seven were square. They were gilt and covered with the same green silk damask as that used for the curtains and, in the usual eighteenth century fashion, when not in use were protected by checked linen-covers. A pair of stools appears in the photograph of the St James's Square side of the Music Room (pl. 29) and these may well represent part of the original set. They look Venetian in style.

In the inventory the chimney-piece is not mentioned, but the mention of a 'Steel stove' should not be taken literally, for in the mid-eighteenth century the word was interchangeable with a grate. It should be noted that the existing basket-grate dates from the early nineteenth century. The two-leaved canvas sliding screen must have stood in front of the fire-place in the winter, but in the summer the 'chimney-board' would have been fitted into the fireplace opening. Frequently these boards (often made simply of canvas on a stretcher) were painted in *trompe l'oeil* to represent a vase of flowers or an architectural perspective and most Turinese chimney-pieces possessed them. The mantelshelf would have been decorated with the four busts, the three groups standing between them forming a *garniture de cheminée*. In front of the fire an oil-cloth – the ancestor of modern linoleum – covered the hearth-slab when not in use, and the rest of the floor was fitted with a Wilton carpet. It is possible that the carpet which is shown in plates 1 and 29 may have been the original mid-eighteenth century one.

The inventory made on the 9th Duke's death in 1777, already referred to, adds a couple of 'India [i.e. lacquer] Back Chairs with Cane Seats', another dining-room table, and a pair of gilt corner-shelves to the contents of the room. Essentially the Norfolk House Music Room must have been a place of parade – a grand entrance into the main suite of state apartments of the house. In mid-eighteenth century England, both in London and the country, the Norfolks, or any grand family, would have lived in the ground-floor rooms when by themselves. For instance, Philip Yorke, when visiting Wolverton in Norfolk in 1750,[79] talks of the Walpole family doing this, leaving the grand first floor for entertaining and the top floor for servants. Lord Hervey called the *piano nobile* at Houghton 'the floor of taste, expense, state and parade'[80] and this graphically sums up what this Norfolk House suite was used for when it was opened.

Music may have been played in the Music Room, but it is odd that no harpsichord is mentioned anywhere in either of the inventories. The stools would probably have been ranged around the walls, more chairs being brought in for card-players when necessary. At large routs refreshments were probably laid out on the dining-room tables, though it is likely that they were folded up when not in use. The 1777 inventory shows that a series of dining-tables was kept on the staircase and landing in the middle of the suite of state rooms of the *piano nobile*. They were probably moved about quite freely on grand occasions, the company eating in the Music Room, the Green Damask Room or the Great Drawing Room as the spirit moved them. Mrs Delany described a ball in honour of the Duke of Cumberland a month or so after the Norfolks' grand opening, and talks of 'suppers' and 'two tables for the dancers, with nothing hot but soups', while mentioning that the Duke's supper was hot, two courses and dessert.[81] This suggests separate dinners in different apartments; and no doubt dancing and card-playing were not specifically restricted to a single room either, for, not counting those in the

pl. 39 The musical trophy in gilded wood superimposed on the
mirror above the chimney-piece in the Music Room

Music Room, a large number of card tables were also inventoried in the Flowered Red Velvet and Great Drawing Rooms. All the four main state rooms of the *piano nobile* had carpets 'to cover the floor', thus they would have had to have been rolled up for a ball. It was not until the nineteenth century that the Great Drawing Room with the 'monkey' doors was turned specifically into a ballroom.

To sum up our conclusions about the decoration of the Music Room: the compartmented ceiling after Inigo Jones and the basic shape of the room are due to the architect Brettingham; the cartouches in the ceiling are attributed to Borra and possibly executed by his Stowe henchman Lovel. Certainly they must be among the finest pieces of English rococo plasterwork extant. Though it is difficult to pin down Borra's role exactly, it seems more or less certain that his was the inspiration behind most of the ornament throughout the Norfolk House schemes. Cuenot, the presumed immigrant French craftsman, executed the *boiseries* and he may have adapted Borra's designs, even restraining Borra's Frenchified Piedmontese *Régence* influence on the three existing walls of the Music Room. It was a considerable tragedy that the fourth window wall, with its superb pier-glasses, was not re-erected in the Museum, for these are so close to Borra's Piedmontese rococo. The whole investigation proves the difficulties of working out the different styles of a single architect and even if the results were a curious conglomeration of English Palladianism, Italian baroque, French *Régence* and Italian rococo, it must be said that the Music Room from Norfolk House is still a magnificent setting and that today the ceiling still makes us gaze in the air as if 'there had been a comet', just as Horace Walpole did in 1756.

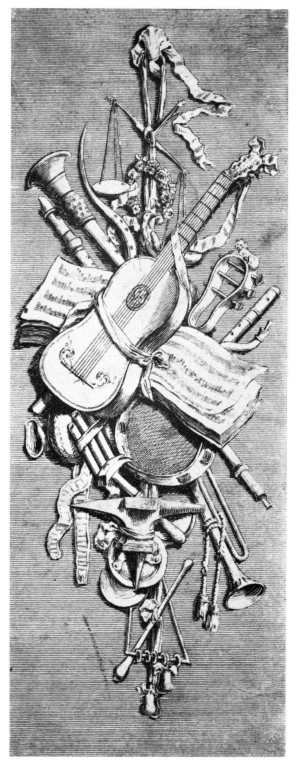

Notes

1 The fullest description of Norfolk House is in F. H. W. Sheppard, ed., *Survey of London*, vol. xxix, 1960, pp. 187–202, and illustrated in vol. xxx, pls. 153–63. See also A. Oswald, in *Country Life*, vol. lxxxii, 25 December 1937, pp. 654-60, and E. B. Chancellor, *The private palaces of London* (1908), pp. 313–23.

2 M. Brettingham, *The plans and elevations of the late Earl of Leicester's house at Holkham*, 1761.

3 Quoted in Sheppard, *op. cit.*, p. 192. Matthew Brettingham's Account Book (P.R.O. C108/362), which includes information about the structural work at Norfolk House, was published by P. E. Howell James, in *Norfolk Archaeology* vol. xxv, pt ii, 1971, pp. 17 ff. The accounts continue to July 1752 and the total came to £18,800. Howell James remarks on the gap between this date and the opening of the house in 1756. He also discusses Brettingham's other works and clients, suggesting that, as Brettingham and the Duke of Norfolk were both freemasons, they may have met in this way. The Duke as Grand Master sponsored Brettingham's son. Brettingham received £100 a year when working at Norfolk House.

4 *Ibid.*, p. 193.

5 Lady Llanover, ed., *The autobiography and correspondence of Mary Granville, Mrs Delany*, 1st ser., vol. iii., 1861, p. 409.

6 Mrs P. Toynbee, ed., *The letters of Horace Walpole*, vol. ii, 1903, p. 396.

7 It was bound up in a scrapbook of newspaper cuttings, etc., which was made by William Farington, recently bought by the Victoria and Albert Museum Library. He was a Captain in the H. E. I. C. S. and by his wife Ann Nash had six children, the eldest of whom became an admiral and lived at Woodvale in the Isle of Wight. For fuller information, see Burke's *Landed Gentry*, vol. i, 1871, pp. 419–20, under Ffarington of Woodvale.

8 She was received at the French Court. Her sister was married in Amsterdam and through her Jacobite sympathies she had further contacts with the Continent. *The Complete Peerage*, vol. ix, p. 632, quotes Lady A. Irwin on the Duchess: '[she] is a sensible woman, and must act the man where talking is necessary... ' Horace Walpole described her on her death in 1773 to Madame du Deffand (W. S. Lewis, ed., *Horace Walpole's Correspondence*, vol. 5 [iii], 1939, p. 361) as follows: 'Le Pape vient de perdre une bien bonne amie, notre Duchesse de Norfolk...femme fausse, intrigante, bigote, très suffisante et très absurde.'

9 Information from the late W. A. Thorpe. A Ms. folio entitled *Worksop Mannor System Proposed for Furnishing the New Building May 1766* seems to have been dictated by the Duchess. It was included among the Arundel Castle Mss. and transferred from the Norfolk Sheffield Estates Office to the custody of the City Librarian. The City Librarian and Miss Rosamund Meredith communicated the contents of the folio to the late W. A. Thorpe. For further information about the Duchess' ornamental designs at Worksop see James Paine's *Plans, elevations and sections of noblemen's houses...*, vol. ii, 1783, pp. 3–5. Mr Marcus Binney will be incorporating further research about the Duchess and her building activities into a series of articles on Worksop for *Country Life*.

10 This suggestion was supported by the appearance of grooves in the face of the brickwork after the panelling was taken down, which suggested that some form of applied wooden framework for paper or fabric had existed before the present panelling was put up. This may well have been the case but, as will be shown, it could have lasted only for a very short time. This information was noted in an article describing the removal of the room to the Museum in the *Cabinet Maker and Complete House Furnisher*, no. 2020, 25 June 1938, p. 435. See also note [76].

11 *Victoria and Albert Museum Bulletin*, vol. ii, no. i, January 1966, pp. 1–11.

12 Quoted in Sheppard, *op. cit.*, p. 192. See also Howell James, *op.cit.*, p. 171.

13 Norfolk Mss., Arundel Castle.

14 Thieme and Becker, *Allgemeines Lexikon der bildenden Künstler*, vol. iv, p. 372 and biographical note in catalogue of the 'Mostra del Barocco Piemontese', 1963, vol. 1, p. 78. See also S. Vesme, *L'arte in Piemonte dal xvi al xviii secolo*, vol. 1, 1963, pp. 177–78. The most convenient list of his works appears in C. Brayda, L. Coli and D. Sesia, *Ingegneri e architetti del sei e settecento in Piemonte*, 1963, pp. 21–2, though no mention of any of his English work appears. Borra started work with B. Alfieri on the Palazzo dell' Accademia Filarmonica (originally the Palazzo Isnardi di Caraglio) in 1740 and continued intermittently there till after Alfieri's death in 1767. He worked for Ludovico Vittorio de Carignano in Turin and at Racconigi between 1752 and 1757, so this must mean that Borra travelled back and forward to Piedmont during the fifties. For a description and photographs of the Palazzo dell'Accademia Filarmonica see M. Bernardi, *Tre palazzi a Torino*, 1963, p. 71 ff.

15 See C. A. Hutton, 'The Travels of "Palmyra" Wood in 1750–1751' in *Journal of Hellenic Studies*, vol. xlvii, 1927, pp. 102–28, and T. H. Clarke, 'The Discovery of Palmyra' in *Architectural Review*, vol. ci, March 1947, pp. 90-6. The suggestion that Borra was a Squire Dorra connected with Lord Charlemont, first made by Maurice Craig and repeated by Dora Wiebenson, *Sources of Greek Revival architecture*, 1969, p. 31, need not be taken seriously. Wiebenson omits any mention of Borra's importance in her study.

16 *The ruins of Palmyra otherwise Tedmore in the desert*, 1753. *The ruins of Balbec otherwise Heliopolis in Coelosyria* came out in 1757. Dawkins is said to have spent £50,000 on publishing these two works.

17 Clarke, *op. cit.*, p. 90. Borra's notebooks are in the possession of the Society for the Promotion of Hellenic Studies.

18 They are all signed 'Borra Arch.us Del.t'. The drawings are in the possession of the R.I.B.A.

19 See C. Hussey, 'Stratfield Saye' in *Country Life*, vol. civ, 10 December 1948, p. 1221. It is the rococo decoration in the drawing room, *loc.cit.*, p. 1165, which Hussey considers Piedmontese in character. Lord Rivers was ambassador in Turin from 1761 to 1768, therefore it is difficult to date Borra's decoration at Stratfield Saye.

20 L. Whistler, 'Signor Borra at Stowe' in *Country Life*, vol. cxxii, 29 August 1957, pp. 390–93. Some of Borra's letters about the garden buildings are amongst the Stowe Mss. in the Huntington Library, San Marino, California. He wrote in French, signing himself 'Très Humble et très Obedient St. [Servant] J. B. Borra'. They date from 1752 to 1754.

21 B. Seeley, *Stowe*, 1763, p. 11.

22 Compare with those shown in *Mostra del barocco piemontese*, vol. iii, 1963, pls. 265–71.

23 Those of the State Bedroom, the Dining Room and Study are

pl. 41 Another ornament by Borra from his *Trattato...*, to be compared with the trophies in the Green Damask Room (see pls. 9 and 30)

pl. 42 One pair of 'Branches, with Nozels, Sockets and pans', part of the decoration in the Music Room

illustrated in Christie's *Catalogue of... the remaining contents of Norfolk House from February 7th–9th*, 1938.

24 See M. Girouard's 'Coffee at Slaughter's', 'Hogarth and his Friends', 'The Two Worlds of St. Martin's Lane' in *Country Life*, vol. cxxxix, 13 January, 27 January and 3 February 1966.

25 R. Gunnis, *Dictionary of British sculpture 1660–1851*, 1953, p. 244.

26 See L. Dickens and M. Stanton, *An eighteenth-century correspondence*, 1910.

27 Plate viii has somewhat similar coffering.

28 Sheppard, *op. cit.*, p. 198.

29 W. Kent, *The designs of Inigo Jones...*, vol. i, 1727, p. 52.

30 Illustrated in Sheppard, *op. cit.*, vol. xxx, pl. 154c.

31 R. Wood, *Palmyra...*, pl. xliii c.

32 *Ibid.*, pl. x c.

33 *Ibid.*, pl. xiii.

34 R. Wood, *Balbec*, pl. xxvii. It should be said that similarly placed heads appear on brackets in Vittone's *Architture civile*, vol. ii, pl. xi. I am indebted to Mrs Barbara Parry for loaning slides of the interior of Racconigi to me. Since this was written N. Gabrielli's *Racconigi*, 1972, has appeared and this illustrates the Salone d'Ercole fully on pp. 47–50. The plasterwork was carried out to Borra's design by Giuseppe Bolina. The Sala di Diana mentioned in the next paragraph is illustrated on p. 51 and again the plasterwork was executed by Bolina. Gabrielli dates all this work between 1755 and 1757.

35 W. and J. Halfpenny, Robert Morris and Thomas Lightoler all contributed to *The modern builder's assistant*, 1742. Figures 80 and 81 there are among the only engraved English rococo eighteenth century designs of this date.

36 Gunnis, *op. cit.*, pp. 111–12.

37 J. Paine, *Plans, elevation, sections and other ornaments of the Mansion House...of Doncaster*, 1751; his other rococo work exists at Nostell, Wadsworth, and Felbrigg, though in execution the plasterwork does not have the lightness of touch found at Norfolk House.

38 Information from Mr Marcus Binney.

39 See J. T. Smith, *Nollekens and his times*, vol. ii, 1828, p. 206.

40 See P. Ward-Jackson, *English furniture designs of the eighteenth century*, Victoria and Albert Museum, 1958, p. 48.

41 See Brayda, Coli, Sesia, *op. cit.*, pp. 10, 20.

42 P. Toynbee, 'Horace Walpole's... visits' in *Walpole Society*, vol. xvi, 1928, p. 19. It is possible that Walpole added this reference to Palmyra later.

43 Some of the documentation for the North Wing at Woburn, dating from 1750–60, is published by G. Scott-Thompson, *Family background*, 1949, pp. 45–54. However, the dating of the decoration of the North Wing is still extremely tentative.

44 Information from Mrs Draper, Archivist to the Bedford Estates Company. I am also indebted to Mr T. Ingram for assistance.

45 Information from Mr Michael J. MacCarthy of Toronto University.

46 Gunnis, *op. cit.*, p. 244. Lovel had Continental contacts, for the elaborate tabernacle of the church of St Jacques at the English College at Douai in France is signed *James Lovell Fecit London*. Information from Rosemary Rendell. (He seems to have spelt his name both with a single and two ls.) He also worked at Crome Court, Worcestershire, and Newenham Paddocks in Warwickshire for Lords Coventry and Denbigh.

47 Mr Michael J. MacCarthy has found various further references to Lovel, and he is at present working on the Stowe Mss.

48 See W. Hawkes, 'Miller's Work at Wroxton' in *Cake and Cockhorse*, Banbury Historical Society, vol. iv, Winter 1969, p. 105 and fig. 17.

49 Dickens and Stanton, *op. cit.*, p. 210.

50 Now demolished. Lovel carved and designed chimney-pieces and crests there in 1757–58. For instance Dacre wrote in 1757 to Miller: 'Lovel has drawn me execrable designs for Gothick Chimneys. I beg you therefore to help me out and send me a little spruce for ye Dressing room and a plainer [one] for ye Bed chamber to be executed in wood: except a slip or block of white marble.' Information from Mr Michael J. MacCarthy. The original references are in the Miller Correspondence in Warwick County Record Office (CR 125 B/455).

51 Dickens and Stanton, *op. cit.*, p. 270. Lovel was also an architect, and he exhibited a design for the Royal Exchange Competition at Dublin in 1769. See H. Colvin *Biographical dictionary of English architects, 1660–1840*, 1954, p. 369.

52 p. 90.

53 Vol. iii, p. 437.

54 Taken from the Drummond's Bank Archives.

55 Duke of Northumberland Accounts in Hoare's Bank Archives and at Alnwick Castle Mss. The sum paid was £48 on 21 March 1752, and may relate to the frames in the Gallery.

56 Duke of Montagu Accounts at Boughton. The sum paid was £6.17s.6d. on 20 February 1759.

57 p. 8. He does not appear listed under Cabinet Makers, and his name is never listed in any of the *Complete guides...of London*. Warwick Street was parallel with the western side of Golden Square and a print by Sutton Nicholls of 1731 shows the street's third floor and dormer windows. See H. Phillips, *Mid-Georgian London*, 1964, p. 236.

58 Rate-book for the Church Warden of the Parish of St James's, Piccadilly, in the Westminster Public Library, Buckingham Palace Road. I am much indebted to Mr Charles Truman for searching these books for me.

59 Norfolk Mss., Arundel Castle.

60 L'Abbé P. Brune, *Dictionnaire des artistes et ouvriers d'art de la France, Franche-Comté*, 1912, pp. 75–6. See also S. Vesme, *op. cit.*, vol. i, p. 380–81.

61 See *Dictionnaire de biographie française*, vol. ix, 1961, p. 1347; G. Daumos, 'Batisseurs de ponts sous Louis XIV' in *Mercure de France*, vol. iii, 1954, pp. 463–73; S. Lamie, *Dictionnaire des sculpteurs de l'école française sous le règne de Louis XIV*, 1906, p. 139.

62 This and another glass between the windows were the only two original mirrors in the Great Room, as a reading of Cuenot's accounts for his work makes clear.

63 See M. Bernardi, *op. cit.*, p. 71 ff., for a full description and illustrations of this palace (originally Isnardi di Caraglio). Bernardi mentions Borra's career and his Middle Eastern travels on p. 120, and calls his style 'Transitional'.
   A close study of part of the gallery (plate xix) indicates a few more similarities to Borra's work at Norfolk House; for instance, the centre of the niche is decorated with a scallop shell in Palmyra fashion and the spirally fluted vase, flanked by two putti, which stands in front of the shell is identical to those on the 'monkey' doors in the Great Drawing Room. Similar flowered *treillage* also can be seen on the top of the niche, on the 'monkey' overdoors and on the canopy of the Stowe State Bed.

64 Victoria and Albert Museum, E.4182–1906 and E.4144–1906.

65 The monogram has been interpreted as being an entwined E and M, standing for the Duke and Duchess' Christian names, Edward and Mary. This is by no means clear.

66 Victoria and Albert Museum, E.616.202–1888.

67 Illustrated in C. P. Curran, *Dublin decorative plasterwork*, 1967, pl. 86. It is essentially a rococo interpretation of the theme and dates from a decade later than that at Norfolk House.

68 C. Hussey, 'Halnaby Hall' in *Country Life*, vol. lxxiii, 8 April 1933, pp. 362–63.

69 Norfolk Mss., Arundel Castle.

70 *Ibid.* These both complement and repeat the names listed in Sheppard, *op. cit.*, p. 192, and are taken from Brettingham's account books. They are recorded at Arundel as follows:—

Cuenot for Carving Gilding	£2643	3	8
Metcalf Upholsterers	£1078	2	4½
Saunders and Bradshaw	£1350	10	1
Edwards Carpenter	£ 713	11	3
Stephens Brasier	£ 519	14	1
Ayray Glasier	£ 50	13	8
Evans Painter	£ 364	11	8½

71 This is Paul Saunders, who specialized in tapestry and upholstery. He was in partnership with George Smith Bradshaw, the cabinet-maker and upholsterer, between 1751 and 1758, when the partnership was dissolved. When in partnership, they had a lease of Carlyle House in Soho Square. See R. Edwards and M. Jourdain, *Georgian cabinet-makers*, 1955, p. 51. Considerable further data exists in the Department of Furniture and Woodwork blue slips on Cabinet-Makers, etc.

72 W. S. Lewis, *op. cit.*, vol. 31, p. 87.

73 See note 22.

74 See D. Owsley and W. Rieder, 'The Glass Drawing Room from Northumberland House' in *Victoria and Albert Museum Yearbook*, no. 2, 1970, p. 109.

75 Alnwick Castle Mss., 121/42, kindly communicated to me by Lady Victoria Percy.

76 This may well tie in with the views stated in note 10. Possibly the Music Room had perfectly plain papered walls and a dado before the new panelling was introduced by Borra and Cuenot, though Metcalfe's bill does not specifically mention work in the Music Room.

77 Norfolk Mss., Arundel Castle.

78 *Ibid.*

79 J. Godber, *The Marchioness Grey of Wrest Park*, 1968, p. 142.

80 W. Ketton Cremer, *Norfolk assembly*, 1957, p. 179.

81 Lady Llanover, *op. cit.*, 1st ser., vol. iii, p. 421.

pl. 44   The Sala da Ricevimènto or di Diana at Racconigi designed by Borra and executed by Giuseppe Bolina. The composition of the door-cases are virtually identical to the 'monkey' doors in the great Drawing Room at Norfolk House (pl. 43). The ceiling also has 'Palmyrene' interlaced circles

pl. 45   A 'monkey' door from Norfolk House standing in Room 48 East in the Museum

pl. 46 (right)   A door from the Green Damask Room. After Norfolk House was demolished one of these was bought by the Art Institute of Chicago

pl. 47   One of a pair of lanterns carved by Cuenot and originally placed over a door on the Grand Staircase in Norfolk House (see pl. 12). Now in the Niarchos Collection in Paris

Appendix A

William Farington's letter has been reproduced with its original spelling and capitalization. Some punctuation and explanatory footnotes have been added.

Surry Street Strand, Feb ye 18th 1756

Dr Isabella & Mary

For this Letter must be address'd to you both, as, I promised in my last Letter to my Mother you shoud have an account of Norfolk House. The Dutchess haveing been so kind to send me a ticket, on opening the Grand Appartment, which as was expected prov'd the finest Assembly ever known in this Kingdom, there were in all eleven rooms Open, three below, the rest above, every room was furnished with a different colour, which used to be reckon'd absurd, but this I Suppose is to be the Standard, as the immense Grandure of the Furniture is scarce to be conceiv'd. Every one alow'd it infinitely superior to any think in this Kindom, & many to most things they had seen in Europe, – but you shall have them as we went along – the Hall is very Plain, on the left hand, you enter a large Room Hung & Furnish'd with a Green Damask, let in with a Handsome Gilt moulding, & several very Fine Paintings on the Hangings, through this into a Wainscotted Room, with Pictures but not very Eligant – then to the Stairs, wch are very large, & the Lights[1] Beautifully Plac'd, 'Twas intirely cover'd with a French Carpet, & in the Angles stood Large China Jarrs with parfumes – the Anti-Chamber was much like the last mention'd Room, tho something Superior, the next Room is large, Wainscotted in a whimsical Taste, the Pannels fill'd with extreem fine Carvings, the Arts & Sciences all Gilt, as well as the Ceiling, which was the same design, here the Dutchess sat, the whole night that she might speak to every one as they came in; having paid yr regards, you then walk forwards; the next Room was Hung & Furnished with Blew-Damask,[2] cover'd with very Fine Paintings, the Gerandoles, fix'd in the Frames of the Pictures, wch had an odd effect, & I can't think will be so good for the Paint, – the next Room a Crimson Damask, no Paintings except over the Chimney, where there is a round Landskip let into the looking Glass which rises from the Chimney to the top of the Room, as do most of the Glasses, the Gerandoles here, are monstrous large, but the Carvings in a Beautiful taste, & being Gilt, have a good Effect upon the Damask, –

you now enter the Great Room, wch is not to be describd, the Tapistry is the finest Picture I ever saw, chiefly with Beasts, it cost in France nine Pounds a Yard, the Hangings just cost nine Hundred Pounds, the Glasses a Thousand, being the largest Plates, I fancy that were ever brought over, but throughout ye whole House the Glass is thought the most remarkable furniture, there are two cristall branches, I don't know what they Cost, – but from what I have seen, imagine about three or four Hundred Pound a Piece, the Furniture Crimson Velvet, in magnificent Gilt Frames, the Chimney Piece white marble, the Festoons as soft, as Gibbons coud work in wood, I don't suppose this room can be out done in Elligance; the next Room is the state Bedchamber 'tis hung & Furnish'd with Blew-Velour except the Bed, wch is Embroidery upon a Peach colour'd French silk, I'm sure I remember it begun near twenty years since, & it is but just now finish'd, neither Baptiste or Honduotre,[3] could paint finer Birds or Flowers, than you'll find in the work; – there is a Brass Rail round it, to prevent People coming too near, the Carvings & Gerandoles in this Room are all Gilt with Pale Gold, wch was vastly admir'd, but to me looks like tarnish'd silver, the next room is intirely Chinese, the Hangings Painted either upon Sattin or Taffity, in the most Beautiful India Pattern you can Imagine, Curtains & Chairs the same, – the Toilet was vastly Magnificent, but I think only Gilt Plate, – on a Chinese Table stood a Basket of French China Flowers, under wch was Room for a Lamp to Burn Perfumes to answer the Flowers, – you now enter the Closset & then you have gone the round, this is furnished with a taffety painted with flowers, it is fill'd with an infinite number of Curiosites, in an Alcove. In the middle stands an India Cabbinet which was set open, to shew four things plac'd in it, ye Prince & Princess of Wales's Pictures, most Curiously ornamented with Brilliants, very, large ones, ye last Supper I took it to be in Amber, a very fine peice of enammell, & an Ivory Ball, just like mine, but I think not so fine a one, ye rest of the curiosities were on each side this Cabbinett in Glass Cases cheifly in Amber, Ivory, China and Japan;[4] the Ceilings are most of them Mosaic, ye Ground Coulr'd the Patterns gilt, there is a vast Profusion of Gilding & a great Shew of Magnificence through ye whole, the marbles are various, but all fine, & great expence in ye workmanship – some being inlaid others in the statuary way. Every one paid their compliments to the Duke in the great Room, & Miss Clifford[5] the Dutchesses niece, stood there, to fix those to Cards, who chose to Play; there was a vast Croud, and a great blase of Diamonds, Lady Granby's[6] were I think the Finest, Lady Rockingham[7] had none at all on, which was not Civil, as every one endeavour'd to make themselves Fine. A Miss Vineyard[8] was thought the Prittest Woman ther, as to Fashions, there was not two Ladies Heads dress'd alike, the more whimsical & absurd the better, the Cloaths on them were all vastly rich; I heard one Single Shop sold above a Hundred Suits, so you judge what Numbers were bought; mine was a Figur'd Velvet of a Pompodore Colour which is the Taste, an intire Silver Clin-Cong[9] Wastecoate, wt a lose Net trimming wav'd over the Skirts & my Hair dress'd French, – dont you think your Brother is growing very youthfull. There was several richer Cloaths, but none I think prittier than my own, I dare say you'll like them – indeed it is thought a very fine suit – it is all Lind with a white Satten; – if I coud have sold my Ticket, it woud have brought a very large sum, for many Fine Folks were just undone about them, but ye Dutchess woud not suffer any but those who visited Her to have them, – a little before this Fine affair I Din'd with the Duke & Dutchess. I'll give you an Account of the Table & then I shall have writ you a long letter with an account of a deal of Fine things; – after a very Elligant Dinner of a great many dishes, in which I discover'd one Fowl. The Table was Prepar'd for Desert, which was a Beautiful Park, round the Edge was a Plantation of Flowering-Shrubs, and in the middle a Fine piece of water, with Dolphins Spouting out water, & Dear dispersd Irregularly over the Lawn, on the Edge of the Table was all the Iced Creams, & wet & dried Sweetmeats, it was such a Piece of work it was all left on the Table till we went to Coffee, – I am greatly oblig'd to them both, as they continue the Civility they always shewd me, – having given me a general invitation, besides sending to me. – Now dont you dream of this Fairy Land, for 'tis almost like it, – but notwithstanding this, I assure you I woud rather be at Home, where I hope to be next month, as early as I can, – Give my Duty to my Mother, my Love to Miss Betty, Mrs. Patten, Mrs. Preston, & as due, & believe me Dear Girls your very affect Bror & Friend

Wm. ffarington.

I Shou'd have told you of Mrs. Spencer's[10] diamond Cap, Her equipage, the Harness of which is Silver –, an Affair I happen'd to see wch diverted me, between Lady Rockingham, Lady Lincoln & Lady Coventry, but of that when we meet. If I can find time I think I must send this account to Bab, write soon –.

This party was the cause of Richard Owen Cambridge's *Elegy Written in an Empty Assembly Room*, published by Dodsley on 11 April 1756, which parodied Pope's *Epistle of Eloisa to Abelard*. Lady Townshend had, unlike Farington, no ticket! For further information, see Richard D. Altick, *Richard Owen Cambridge, belated Augustan*, 1941, p. 125.

In scenes where Hallet's Genius has combin'd
With Bromwich[11] to amuse and chear the Mind;
Amid this Pomp of Cost, this Pride of Art,
What mean these Sorrows in a Female Heart?
Ye crowded Walls, whose well enlighten'd Round
With Lovers sighs and Protestations sound,
Ye Pictures flatter'd by the learn'd and wise,
Ye Glasses ogled by the brightest Eyes,
Ye Cards, whom Beauties by their Touch have blest,
Ye Chairs, which Peers and Ministers have prest,
How are ye chang'd! like you my Fate I moan,
Like you, alas! neglected and alone –
For ah! to me alone no Card is come,
I must not go abroad – and cannot *Be at Home*.

But when no Cards the Chimney-Glass adorn,
The dismal Void with Heart-felt Shame we mourn;
Conscious Neglect inspires a sullen Gloom,
And brooding Sadness fills the slighted Room.
If some happier Female's Card I've seen
I swell with Rage, or sicken with the Spleen;
While artful Pride conceals the bursting Tear,
With some forc'd Banter of affected Sneer;
But now grown desp'rate, and beyond all Hope,
I curse the Ball, the Duchess and the Pope.[12]

O! could I on my waking brain impose,
Or but forget at least my present woes!
Forget 'em – how! – each rattling coach suggests
The loath'd ideas of the crowding guests.
To visit – were to publish my disgrace;
To meet the spleen in ev'ry other place;
To join old maids and dowagers forlorn;
And be at once their comfort and their scorn!
For once to read – with this distemper'd brain,
Ev'n modern novels lend their aid in vain.
My mandoline – what place can music find
Amid the discord of my restless mind?
How shall I waste this time which slowly flies!
How to lull to slumber reluctant eyes!
This night the happy and th'unhappy keep
Vigils alike, – Norfolk *has murder'd sleep*.

1   Cuenot's lanterns over the doors. See Appendix D, 3.
2   Farington must have been mistaken, for the room was hung with green damask. Perhaps this green damask would have appeared blue in the candlelight.
3   Jean-Baptiste Monnoyer and Melchior de Hondecoeter.
4   Many of these items were sold in the Norfolk House sale at Christie's on 7, 8, 9 February 1938.
5   The Duchess' sister, Elizabeth, married Lord Clifford of Chudleigh, and Farington must refer to their daughter Mary, who later married Sir Hugh Smythe, Bart, of Acton Burnell. The Countess of Kildare, writing to her husband on 27 May 1757 (B. FitzGerald, ed., *Correspondence of Emily, Duchess of Leinster*, vol. i, 1949, pp. 38-9), mentioned that 'Lady Caroline Keppel had a letter from Miss Clifford, who lives with the Duchess of Norfolk, in which she mentions a man having been found in the King of France's closet, with a knife hid under his cloths. He certainly will be murderd at last.'
6   Lady Frances Seymour, daughter of the 6th Duke of Somerset. Her husband became 3rd Duke of Rutland. *The Complete Peerage*, vol. xi, p. 269, quotes Horace Walpole's remarks about her extravagance; she and her sister 'squandered seven thousand pounds a piece in all kinds of baubles and frippery' in 1749.
7   Mary, daughter of Thomas Bright and wife of Charles Watson-Wentworth, 2nd Marquess of Rockingham. She was famous for her diamonds; for instance, Lady Harcourt wrote, on 6 February 1755, describing a masquerade: 'Lady Rockingham and Lady Coventry, were covered with diamonds: the former represented Night, and the stars upon her dress, it's said, were real jewells...' See E. W. Harcourt, *The Harcourt Papers*, vol. iii, n. d., p. 67.
8   Undoubtedly, Mary Wynyard, who married, on 8 August 1756, John 2nd Earl De la Warr. *The Complete Peerage*, vol. ii, p. 163, quotes the *Gentleman's Magazine*, saying she was 'a remarkable beauty'. She had a fortune of £10,000.
9   Clinquant – a gaudy, silver-thread brocaded decoration.
10 Her husband was not created Earl Spencer until 1765. Mrs Delany (Lady Llanover), *op. cit.*, 1st ser., vol. iii, pp. 399–402, describes her famous diamonds 'worth twelve thousand pounds'.
11 The well-known cabinet-maker William Hallet and the wall-paper manufacturer Thomas Bromwich. See R. Edwards. *op. cit.*, p. 49. They did not in fact have anything to do with Norfolk House.
12 A reference to the Norfolks' catholicism.

Appendix B

The extract from Cuenot's bill for 'Sundry Articles of Work done and Goods delivered, from March 5th 1753 to Feb 24th 1756', relating to the Music Room (Arundel Castle Mss.)

Musick Room

	£	s	d
To carving 9 heads with various Ornaments to fold over mouldings with flowers & 4 modillions	21	3	0
To carving the Ornaments over 3 Doors	30	10	0
To carving 6 Trophies to go in the pannels with laurels & oak branches	60	5	0
To carving 8 Ears for D°	8	18	0
To 8 Branches of flowers for D° not design'd in the Drawing	4	2	0
To carving the Ornaments of 6 less pannels with foldridge & flowers	39	12	0
To carving the sides of two Glass frames with flowers folding over Sticks	16	9	0
To carving the two bottoms of D° not express'd in the Drawing	6	15	0
To carving 54 foot of Raffled leaf & stick for the Window Cornishes at 1^s p foot	2	14	0
To 54 foot of lonf water leaf for D° @ 1^s 5^d p foot	3	16	6
To 54 foot of Bead beaded @ 5^d p foot	1	2	6
To making the Scrowls of D° & to four large pannels at the top & bottom & to the top of the two Glasses	9	8	0
To making the mouldings of 5 pannels and the top of 2 Doors which makes 16 pieces	8	12	0
To carving an Ornament to cover the joint of the Chimney Glass	4	18	0
carried forward	£235	1	0

	£	s	d
Musick Room Bro^t forward	£235	1	0
To carving 11 different pattern mouldings for the Cornish of the top of the Room &c.			
To 108 feet of Bubble & floroon @ 1^s 2^d p foot	6	6	0

	£	s	d
To 108 feet of fluting for D° @ 11^d p foot	4	19	0
To 287 feet of french Eggs & Darts for the great pannels @ 1^s p foot	14	7	0
To 313 feet of Ribbon & Stick for D° @ 4^d p foot	5	4	4
To 299 feet of Water leaf for the in & outsides of two pannels @ 8^d p foot	9	19	4
To 42 feet of large Beads for the Cornishes of D° @ 6^d p foot	1	1	0
To 26 feet of french Eggs & Darts for the top of the Glass of D° @ 1^s p foot	1	6	0
To 499 feet 6 inches of italion foldridge on streight mouldings @ 10^d p foot	10	16	3
To 271 feet of D° on sweep mouldings @ D°	11	5	10
To 499 feet of Beads & pearls & 6 inches on streight mouldings @ 5^d p foot	10	7	11
To 271 feet of D° on sweep mouldings @ D°	5	12	11
To 83 feet of large Beads for the Cornish over the pannels & the tops of the Glass frames @ 6^d p foot	2	1	6
To carving 180 feet of italion foldridge round the impost @ 9^d p foot	6	15	0
To 180 feet of Beads & pearls for D° @ 5^d p foot	3	15	0
To carving the plints of the bottom of two Glass frames with Scrowls & floroons 11 feet @ 1^s 6^d p foot	16	6	0
To making, carving, & guilding 12 Double Branches with Nozels, Sockets & pans	57	12	0
To guilding the two Glass frames	18	8	0
To guilding 7 heads with Ornaments	2	12	0
To guilding the Ornaments of the three pannels over the three Doors	9	6	0
To guilding 6 large Trophies of Musick	20	15	0
To guilding the 4 large foldridge leaves at the bottom of the pannels	6	18	0
To guilding 8 Ears for the great pannels	3	3	0
To guilding the Ornaments of 6 small pannels top & bottom	16	18	0
To guilding 3329 feet of 11 Different patterns of Mouldings	55	9	8
To guilding the Cieling	35	7	0

	£	s	d
To guilding the Cornish & Architraves of D°	28	5	o
To guilding the imposts Bass, Window shutters & architraves of the Windows & Doors	21	7	o
To guilding & painting 11 small Stools	12	2	o
To guilding & painted 7 larger	13	14	o
To jointing 3 feet 6 inch. of Bass for the sides of the Chimney after it was fix'd		3	6
To 19 feet 7 inches of leaf Grass to the impost @ 4ᵈ p foot		6	6
To carving a Freeze for the top of the Door	1	10	o
To carving a Freeze with Band & flowers for the Door of the Great Room	1	16	o
	£645	7	3

Appendix C

These lists of the contents of the Music Room are extracted from the two complete inventories of Norfolk House. The cover of the earlier one is labelled: 'Inventory of Furniture in St. James's Square when rebuilt and new furnish't' (i. e. 1756). The first page is headed: 'Inventory of Furniture at his Grace the Duke of Norfolk's, St. James's Square'. (Both inventories are in the Arundel Castle Mss.)

No 21   Musick Room.
3 Green and Silk Damask W^d Curtains Carved & Gilt Cornices
4 brass Rods Down the Sides
2 Large pier Glasses
2 brass Rods before Do
A Large Glass over Chymney
6 pr Rich Double Arms Gilt
A Card Table covered with Velvett the frame Gilt
2 Mahogany Carved Compass front Card tables
14 Stools Different Sizes, Green & Gold frames covered with damask & Checque cases
A 2 leaved Canvas Sliding screen
A Steel stove, Shovell, tongs, poker, fender & brush, Steel Coving & Chimney boards
4 Bronze Busts
3 Groups do
A Mahog^y Dining table
A Wilton Carpett to cover the floor
3 brown holland Spring Curtains
An oil Cloth lined with bays to Cover hearth

The second inventory is labelled 'An Inventory of the Household Goods and Furniture...at Norfolk House... bequeathed by the Will of Edward late Duke of Norfolk to remain as Heir Looms in his Family...1777'. Edward, Duke of Norfolk, the rebuilder of Norfolk House, died on 20 September 1777. His Duchess had died four years earlier on 27 May 1773. As they had no children, the Howard properties, including Norfolk House, were inherited by the Duke's second cousin, Charles Howard of Greystoke, Cumberland, whom Horace Walpole (W. S. Lewis, op. cit., vol. 30, 1961, p. 241), noted was 'mad, is ill with the Duke and Duchess, and has only one cub of a son', in 1767. Elizabeth Noel (M. Elwin, ed., The Noels and the Milbankes, 1967, pp. 91-2) wrote to her aunt in 1778 describing another ball at Norfolk House under the regime of this Duke and his Duchess: 'We went there at 9 o'clock & even then found every room brim-full. I don't know whether you have seen the old Duchess – she is a fat little vulgar figure, but as I only saw her two minutes during the Evening I should not recollect her. [She was Catherine, daughter and co-heir of John Brockholes of Claughton, Lancs.] The House is superb, consisting of 8 or 9 Rooms en Enfilade; 6 of them are immensely large, there are some very fine Pictures, amazing large Glasses and one room is hung with white Sattin, & velvet flowers upon it. There is a State Bedchamber & a large Crucifix. They danced, tho' none but vulgars, & in another room there were Refreshments. Every Person of Quality, Fashion & the Ton were there (excepting the House of Commons members) besides a great many Giggs, in all about 7 or 800...It was very hot & very crowded; besides Roman Catholics in abundance, there were all the Blood of all the Howards... It was dreadful getting away, I scream'd finely, several chairs were broken to pieces.'

No 21. Musick Room.
One Stool 9 ft 4 long – 2 Do 8 ft long – 2 Do 7 ft 8 long – 2 Do 5 ft 6 long – 7 small square Stools all Covered with Green Silk Damask & check Cases and Green & Gold Frames – 2 India Back Chairs with Cane Seats – 2 large Pier Glasses in Carv'd & Gilt Frames 7 ft by 4 ft Two Head Plates 2 ft 4 high – Chimney Glass with Border 3 ft 7 by 4 ft 1 wide – head plate 2 ft 2 High 2 Small Head Plates & 8 Pieces in Border – 12 Rich Carved & Gilt Girandoles for 2 lights each – 4 Upright brass Rods to windows – 2 Gardes before Glasses – 3 Old Spring Curtains – 3 Carv'd & Gilt Window Cornishes – 2 Carved Mahog'y Card Tables – A Plain do – Oval mahogany Dining Table – Square Ditto – Two Corner Shelves with Carved & Gilt Moldings.

Appendix D

As a result of the discovery of Cuenot's bill, it seems worth while publishing the relevant sections which relate to surviving Norfolk House woodwork, and to pieces of woodwork and furniture shown in the photographs illustrating this monograph and to those of the interior of the house before its demolition.

1 The 'monkey' doors (pl. 43)
In the Christie's sale catalogue of 1938, all the woodwork, doorways, etc., from the Great Drawing Room were sold in one lot,[1] and the four 'monkey' doors were there mentioned as being 'moulded in gilded plaster work'. The *Survey of London*,[2] describing this room as the Saloon or Ballroom, considered that 'only its form and such minor details as the simple pedestal of the walls and the mahogany six-panelled doors were of the eighteenth century', and they go on to suggest that all its 'sumptuous' decoration in the 'Louis Quinze' style was done at the time of the renovation of the house in 1845, citing that much of the enrichment, including no doubt the doorcases, were modelled or cast in papier-mâché or *carton pierre*. We have already considered the ceiling entablature and the mantelpiece in the main body of this monograph and Cuenot's bill clearly shows that the pier-glass, or 'Trumo', between the windows, the 'Chimney Trumo' (see pl. 8), and two of the doors are also original. However, all the other mirrors and their elaborate frames, including the two visible on either side of the mantelpiece in plate 8, the typically French *Régence* panels, the monogram panel over the doors, and two of the doors themselves were all made up in papier-mâché and plaster at the time of the renovation. Obviously Christie's were unlucky in cataloguing the door they had tested, for two of them were wood and two plaster.

All this nineteenth century decoration needs a little explanation: William Farington (see Appendix A) thought the room 'not to be described' and shows that all the walls were hung with tapestry imported from France. The 1756[3] inventory of the house calls it the 'Tapistry Room' and lists 'A sett of rich tapistry hangings' and the two mirrors, but, by the date of the second inventory of 1777, the tapestries had been removed and replaced by 'Red and White Paper'. Presumably this had become shabby and inadequate by the mid-nineteenth century and additional mirrors and ornamentation were therefore put up.

The 'monkey' doors were considered for a long time as being of mid-nineteenth century date, so it is satisfactory that the bill, the inventories, coupled with the fact of the

similar doors by Borra at Racconigi (pl. 44), completely prove Borra's authorship and further strengthen the case for Borra being the master mind behind all the Norfolk House decoration, with the exceptions already sifted out. For further reference see note 34 of the main text.

One of the 'monkey' doors is now in the Untermyer Collection in New York[4] and the other was bought by this Museum in 1960 and has recently been put on view in Room 48 East (pl. 45).

Borra also used an identical spirally fluted vase in some of his decoration in Turin[5] and the flowered grill-work or *treillage* is extremely Piedmontese in character. They are also completely alien to any contemporary English work and only bear a vague similarity to some of the engravings of another Italian, Gaetano Brunetti.[6]

Cuenot's bill for the two doorcases is quoted as follows:

	£	s	d
Great Room			
To Carving 63 feet of Eggs Darts & bands for the architraves of the Doors @ 1ˢ 2ᵈ p foot	3	13	6
To 63 feet of Sprigs & flowers in a hollow of Dᵒ @ 1ˢ 6ᵈ p foot	4	14	6
To 63 feet of Beads for Dᵒ @ 6ᵈ p foot	1	11	6
To 39 feet of water leaf for Dᵒ @ 1ˢ p foot	1	19	0
To 26 feet of italion foldridge in a pannel over the Doors aside the Mosaick @ 10ᵈ p foot	1	1	8
To 35 feet of eggs on the Rake to the Cornishes of dᵒ under the Monkies @ 9ᵈ p foot	1	6	3
To 35 feet of fluting for Dᵒ @ 8ᵈ p foot	1	2	6
To a Streight foldridge ornament with rakes 32 feet of raffled leaf @ 2ˢ 6ᵈ p foot	4	0	0
To 6 feet of Eggs & tongues on the pediment @ 8ᵈ		4	0
To 5 feet 6 inches of Cups & balls for Dᵒ @ 6 p foot		2	9
To cutting & shaping the 4 Cornishes & running all the moulding by hand & working it to the profile	2	5	0
	£22	0	8

	£	s	d
To Carving 3 members of the 2 Cornishes for D° in mahogany the same as to the 4 Doors of the other Rooms	2	1	11
To forming & carving the middle Modillion with Frames head & a floroon with berries at bottom	3	5	0
To Carving 2 pieces of Mosaick with flowers a top	2	1	6
To turning 2 Vauzes carv'd with four different Ornaments	3	10	0
To two Palm Trees for the top of the Vauzes of D°	3	0	0
To carving four Monkies in different postures	19	12	0
To Carving 4 large festoons of fruit & flowers supported by the Monkies measure 24 feet	17	6	0
To Carving 4 small pannels a side the Doors		2	0
To Guilding all the Ornaments & architraves of the Doors	31	16	0
	£104	15	1

The problem, which cannot now be solved with any certainty, is where Borra's two original doors stood in the room: did they either frame the doors to the Service Stairs and the State Dressing Room (i. e. on the mantelpiece wall) or were they set in the wall next to the Flowered Velvet Room (see plan, pl. 4)? One of those shown in plate 43 must be a plaster copy. A possibility that the left-hand door in this photograph is the original is suggested by the elaborately carved festoon in a panel in the corner to the right of the door. It looks like Cuenot's carving, though I have been unable to find the charge for it in his bill.

2 Doorcase

One of the doorcases from the Green Damask or Flowered Velvet Rooms (pl. 46) is now in the Art Institute of Chicago.[7] These two rooms were thrown into one in the early part of this century and there were originally five of these Italianate creations carved by Cuenot in these rooms.[8] A mask-cartouche flanked by festooned garlands centred these compositions and their architraves formed pedestals for picture frames above (pl. 9). The mask-cartouche is similar to those in the Music Room (pl. 33) and this door was also designed by Borra, as it is comparable to examples in the Palazzo dell'Accademia Filarmonica.[9] The relevant section of Cuenot's bill is as follows:–

Green middle Room

	£	s	d
To carving 17 feet 6 inches of Bubble & floroon for the top of the Doors @ 13 d p foot		18	11½
To 17 feet of Water leaf for D° @ 10 d p foot		14	2
To 17 feet & ½ of Bubble & tongue in a hollow for D° @ 11 d p foot		16	0½
To 18 feet & ½ of Band & floroon for D° @ 1 s 3 d p foot	1	3	1½
To carving a Daina's head	1	1	0
To carving a Shell on D° joining to ya ornament	1	12	0
To carving two festoons which proceeds from the Shell, & joins in two small pannels	2	0	0
To guilding all D°	4	6	0
	£12	11	3½

3 Lanterns

In plate 12 it is possible to see one of a pair of lanterns that served as over-door lights in the lower part of the staircase hall. These are the 'Lights' that William Farington considered 'Beautifully Plac'd' (Appendix A) and they were sold in the 1938 sale and illustrated in Christie's catalogue (pl. 47).[10] Messrs Blairman had them in 1956 and they are now in the Niarchos Collection in Paris. Cuenot charged as follows:–

	£	s	d
To carving 2 illuminating lanthorns with an Eagle at the top of each, & a head in the middle	26	12	6
To lining D° with tinn	3	5	0

4 Pier-tables, etc.

The pier-tables decorated with masks of Mercury between the windows of the Green Damask Room are clearly shown in plate 30, and were also sold in the Christie's sale.[11] Cuenot billed them as follows:–

	£	s	d
To carving two Tables with three heads & different Ornaments & a bottom Rail to each	48	12	0

Cuenot carved two similar 'Tables' and 'Girandoles for the Corner of the Room' in the Flowered Velvet Room next door. His most expensive single piece was 'A Table with ornament cut through, 3 heads, festoons of Drapery, & a Trophy with festoons of flowers & a Rail between the legs with a Monkey on it', obviously to match the Monkey doors in the Great Drawing Room. This came to £35.4s.6d.[12]

5 Pier-glasses and Overmantels

As plates 30 and 9 so clearly show the pier-glasses and overmantels in the Green Damask Room and as Cuenot's bill for a doorcase and the table in this room have already been extracted in sections 2 and 3, the bill for these items are also reproduced:

Green Middle Room

	£	s	d
To carving a Trumo between the Window as follows			
To a Freeze at the bottom of D°	2	3	6
To carving the plint of D° with a sanded fret	1	2	0
To carving a Montons to cover the joints of the Glass with ornamented leaves & a stick with flowers folding over D° 22 feet	4	12	0
To the Ornament at the bottom of the pillaster	1	8	0
To 2 others D° with a Shell, a palmette, & festoons of flowers & a Bunch of D° 3 feet by 8 inches & ½ with a Mathematical Trophie, a laurel branch & an Oak branch tied with a ribbon	6	18	0
To carving a Mercury's head wth ornaments a top	1	7	0
To carving the ornaments to go over the heads with sweeping festoons of flowers, with various foldridge 4 feet by 3 feet 6	7	5	0
To carving 34 feet of double twisted ribbon with a hollow in the middle to cover the joint of the Glass @ 1ˢ p foot	1	14	0
To carving the top side leaves 34 feet @ 10ᵈ p foot	1	8	4
To guilding the foremention'd Work	10	8	0
	38	5	10
To carving & guilding another Trumo D°	38	5	10
	£76	11	8

	£	s	d
To carving a chimney frame for a picture in the middle with Cups & balls 13 feet 6 inch @ 9½		10	8¼
To 13 feet 6 inches of Water leaf for the top of D° @ 1ˢ p foot		13	6
To carving 2 foldridge ornaments to the top of the Round with Drops of flowers	2	15	0
To carving & guilding all the other ornaments belonging to the same chimney piece	38	5	10

1 Christie's, *op. cit.*, p. 63, lot 286.
2 Sheppard, *op. cit.*, p. 198.
3 The splendid chandeliers noticed by William Farington are described as '2 Glass Lustres 24 lights each, Chairs etc 7 Brown holland and paper Cases to do'. Various other pieces of furniture, such as 'Carved and gilt stands', 'Glass Girandoles' and even the chimney-piece, all had leather covers or cases for protection.
4 See Y. Hackenbroch, *English furniture from the Irwin Untermyer Collection*, 1958, p. 77, pls. 334-35.
5 See note 63 of the main text. Vases on consoles appear as overdoor decoration in the Palazzo dell'Accademia Filarmonica. See M. Bernardi, *op. cit.*, fig. xv.
6 *Sixty different sorts of ornaments...very usefull to painters, sculptors, stone-carvers, wood-carvers, silversmiths, etc.*, 1736.
7 See B. Wriston, 'The Howard Van Doren Shaw Memorial Collection' in *Museum Studies*, The Art Institute of Chicago, 1969, pp. 96–9.
8 E. B. Chancellor, *op. cit.*, fig. opposite p. 323, illustrates the Green Damask Room before the wall was removed. This also proves that the connecting doors were moved to the chimney wall. In the Arundel Castle Mss., there are a series of picture lists showing the positions of pictures, doors, etc., and the plan for the 'Green Room on the first floor' clearly shows no doors on this wall. Therefore the door connecting with the Grand Stair Case must also have been a later insertion.
9 See M. Bernardi, *op. cit.*, fig. xvi. The principle of using a framed painting as an overdoor is also similar.
10 Christie's, *op. cit.*, plate opposite p. 56, lot 264.
11 *Ibid.*, lot 221.
12 Plate 8 shows four elaborate pier-tables but it is impossible to connect any of them with any certainty with Cuenot's work mentioned in his bills for furnishing this room.